DARINA ALLEN is Ireland's best-known food ambassador. She has run the world-renowned Ballymaloe Cookery School in Shanagarry, Co. Cork, situated in the middle of a 100-acre organic farm, since 1983. Darina is the bestselling author of nineteen books including *Ballymaloe Cookery Course, Forgotten Skills of Cooking*, which won the André Simon award in 2009, *One Pot Feeds All, Simply Delicious: The Classic Collection, Irish Traditional Cooking* and *Grow, Cook, Nourish*. She presented nine series of her cookery programme, *Simply Delicious*, shown on television around the world and writes a weekly food column for the *Irish Examiner*. Darina is a tireless campaigner for local produce, founded the first farmers' markets in Ireland and is a leading Irish member of the Slow Food movement. She is a natural teacher, whose enthusiasm and energy for good things is contagious, and has won many awards, including the Guild of Food Writers' Lifetime Achievement award 'for her incalculable contribution to culinary education'.

www.cookingisfun.ie
@ballymaloecookeryschool
@darina_allen

DARINA ALLEN: HOW TO COOK

The **100** essential recipes everyone should know

PHOTOGRAPHY BY NASSIMA ROTHACKER

KYLE BOOKS

For all the heroic teachers and activists who are battling to have practical cooking and growing skills embedded in the national curriculum.

An Hachette UK Company
www.hachette.co.uk

First published in Great Britain in 2021
by Kyle Books, an imprint of
Octopus Publishing Group Limited
Carmelite House
50 Victoria Embankment
London EC4Y 0DZ
www.kylebooks.co.uk
www.octopusbooksusa.com

ISBN: 978-0-85783-965-7

Distributed in the US by
Hachette Book Group,
1290 Avenue of the Americas,
4th and 5th Floors,
New York, NY 10104

Distributed in Canada by
Canadian Manda Group,
664 Annette St., Toronto, Ontario,
Canada M6S 2C8

Publisher **Joanna Copestick**
Project editor **Vicky Orchard**
Editorial assistant **Jenny Dye**
Design **Helen Bratby**
Illustrations **Lydia Hugh-Jones**
Photography **Nassima Rothacker**
Food styling **Annie Rigg**
Props styling **Morag Farquhar**
Production **Allison Gonsalves**

A Cataloguing in Publication record for this title is available from the British Library

Printed and bound in China

10 9 8 7 6 5 4 3 2 1

CONTENTS

INTRODUCTION

··

The working title of this book was '100 recipes no one should leave school without'. Whether you decide to be an astronaut, an architect, a doctor or engineer, we all need to be able to cook in order to feed ourselves properly. Otherwise we are completely at the mercy of other people for our sustenance.

So much depends on the food we eat: our health, our energy, our vitality and our ability to concentrate. It's the 'fuel' we put in the 'tank' to keep us going. It's crucially important to think about the quality, it doesn't have to be expensive but cheapness should not be the only criteria. In fact, nowadays, many of us know more about the lives of celebrities than how our food is produced. So much depends on dinner that it's vital to take all these things into consideration when you go shopping, plus animal welfare, food miles and other environmental issues.

So, why is it important to be able to cook? Apart from being in control of your own health, it also means you can travel anywhere in the world and get a job. It's the easiest way to win friends and influence people – you will never be short of guests if you can rustle up a meal at a moment's notice. Infinitely better for your wallet and your waistline. We are what we eat...

If you start with good-quality ingredients, you need to do so little to make them taste good. If you don't, you need to be a magician to make something delicious and that's where all the foams and skidmarks on plates come in to distract and compensate for the fact that the flavour wasn't there in the first place.

The secret of all good food is 'mindful' shopping. Most people in their busy lives don't give a moment's thought to how food is produced, where it comes from or whether it is in season. I'm very fortunate to live in the midst of a small organic farm where we have our own gardens and greenhouses so we know the source of a lot of the food we eat. But even if you live in an urban area, you can choose to grow some salad leaves, radishes or pea shoots on your windowsill. Tomatoes, cucumbers, courgettes and beans can be grown on a balcony or roof and most cities now have one or several farmers' markets where you can buy fresh, seasonal produce directly from farmers and food producers. Remember all good food starts in rich, fertile soil. Our food should be our medicine rather than bottles of vitamins and supplements.

The basic skills of home cooking are by far the most important. It's really not difficult to learn how to cook but many people convince themselves that it's way beyond them. It's so worth developing a repertoire of simple, delicious recipes that you can build on and have fun creating variations, not just returning to the same few dishes over and over again. If you can cook, you will know exactly what's in your food. A loaf of bread will have three or four ingredients as opposed to 19 or 20, many of which may not even be mentioned on the label.

This book is a collection of essential recipes that both beginners and experienced cooks need to know. Recipes you'll find yourself turning to over and over again, from traditional to more modern classics, incorporating flavours from around the world. Recipes that deliver on taste but also teach basic skills that are the foundation of all kinds of creations. **Everyday Staples** are the recipes that will form the backbone of your cooking, from sauces and a simple green salad to baking a loaf of bread or creating your own stock.

COVID-19 has definitely been a game changer. During the first lockdown, several high-achieving friends who could 'run the country' suddenly found themselves working from home with none of the usual back-up or support. They were faced with the reality of having to provide 21 meals a week for their family but could scarcely make toast. In 'real' life, the kids were dropped off at the crèche and playschool on their way to work, then picked up in their jammies on the way home. At the weekends, the whole family ate out, so no need to cook. A highly successful CEO of a multinational company was in tears on the end of the phone – she scarcely knew how to shop for food, not to mention cook it.

Time to make some fundamental changes in our educational system. We've failed several generations of young people by not emphasizing the importance of acquiring life as well as academic skills. The strong subliminal message since the 1960s has been that practical skills are of lesser value and consequently several generations have left our homes and schools without the basic life skills to feed themselves properly. They are convinced that it's drudgery, that they can't do it, and so they miss out on the fun and satisfaction of being able to rustle up a meal in minutes for family and friends from a few inexpensive ingredients.

Everyone is so crazy busy nowadays trying to keep all the balls in the air – studying, commuting, home-schooling. Day-to-day life is super hectic, feeding fussy kids, picky eaters, ravenous teenagers, dropping kids off to music lessons, play dates, matches – not to mention actual food shopping – so you'll need to make a basic survival plan. Batch cooking needs to be part of the equation. Slow cookers are a godsend, not expensive and mean that for just a few minutes' work in the morning, a delicious meal in one pot can be ready to pop on the table when you all arrive home in the evening.

I'm anti-gadget, but if you are going to cook, you'll need a bit of basic kitchen kit. Check out the **Essential Kitchen Equipment** (page 10). Start with essentials, but choose each item so it will last a lifetime – a sturdy chopping board, a heavy, stainless-steel saucepan, a few good knives and don't leave the shop without a steel and learning how to sharpen them.

Every cook needs a well-stocked storecupboard so they can rustle up meals in minutes. Make clever use of your freezer because food will, of course, freeze forever but be aware that the quality and flavour gradually deteriorate, so try to keep track. Reckon to do a monthly stock-take of the contents of your freezer. Maybe have a Freezer Feast every 2-3 weeks where absolutely everything for that meal comes from the freezer, using up any snacks, meat or pre-prepped ingredients. It's also worth having lots of single portions and snacks in there that can be defrosted quickly when family members arrive home at random times. Make full use of shortcuts like frozen puff and shortcrust pastry. I'm a bit of a purist but even though I no longer have four kids to get out to school every day, I'm acutely aware of the day-to-day pressures of family life.

In many ways, this book is a call to arms – to bump the food we eat and feed to our families right up to the top of the agenda. Join me in demanding that practical cooking and growing skills be embedded in the national curriculum from kindergarten upwards for the future health of our nations.

THE BASICS

INGREDIENTS

ESSENTIAL KITCHEN EQUIPMENT

USE-BY, SELL-BY & BEST BEFORE DATES

STORECUPBOARD

Flour – plain, self-raising, strong brown, strong white, coarse brown

Baking powder/bicarbonate of soda/ fast-action yeast

Oatmeal and porridge oats

Pasta – spaghetti, macaroni, penne etc

Noodles - rice and egg

Grains – couscous, bulgur wheat, quinoa, freekeh, pearl barley

Rice – basmati, arborio, Thai fragrant

Canned fish – sardines, tuna, mackerel, anchovies

Canned vegetables – tomatoes, sweetcorn

Canned beans – chickpeas, kidney beans, black-eyed beans, cannellini beans

Oils – extra virgin, grapeseed, groundnut, sunflower, sesame

White and red wine vinegar

Sea salt – local or Maldon

Chilli flakes, Piment d'Espelette, Aleppo pepper

Whole spices – coriander, cardamom, nutmeg, cumin, cloves, cinnamon

English mustard powder

Sauces – soy, fish, sweet chilli, oyster, plum, hot sauce, harissa

Tapenade

Chicken stock (a standby if you don't have homemade stock)

Nuts – hazelnuts, walnuts, almonds, cashews, pecans, pistachios

Dried fruit

Good-quality chocolate

Homemade jam and marmalade

Honey

Ballymaloe tomato relish

Cream crackers or Carr's water biscuits

Eggs – organic and free range

Garlic

Onions and potatoes

Carrots

INGREDIENTS

If you want to be able to whizz up meals in minutes, you need to ensure that your storecupboard is always well stocked. Everyone's priorities will be different but the following are some suggestions for items that I find invaluable.

FRIDGE

Butter
Cheese – mature Cheddar,
  Parmesan, halloumi, feta, paneer
Salami and/or chorizo
Dijon mustard
Thai curry paste
Olives

FREEZER

Good ice-cream
Frozen fruit – raspberries,
  blackcurrants, gooseberries, etc
Tortillas
Pitta bread

A FEW TREATS

Salted capers
Truffle oil
Gentleman's Relish
  (Patum Peperium)
Panforte di Siena

GOOD TO KNOW ✳ GUIDELINES FOR RICE & PASTA PORTIONS

People's idea of a portion can
vary wildly but here are my
suggested guidelines:
Basmati rice 50–65g (2–2½oz)
uncooked rice per person
Dried pasta (fettuccine/
spaghetti) 50–75g (2–3oz)
per person
Fresh pasta 100–125g
(3½–4½oz) per person
Filled pasta 150–175g (5–6oz)
per person

HERBS

Fresh herbs are an integral part of
my cooking. Flicking through this
book, you'll find that virtually every
recipe includes one or several
herbs. They add a pop of flavour
and a delicious freshness. We grow
more than 50 herbs at Ballymaloe
– some annuals, like basil,
coriander, dill and annual marjoram
– and many trusty perennials that
sleep for the winter and pop up
again in spring or those like thyme,
rosemary and sage that are hardy
throughout winter and add gutsy
flavour to robust cold-weather
casseroles, stews and braises.

These are my top six herbs – if
I had a little more space, I would
definitely have included French
tarragon and lovage, both
perennials, and Genovese basil in
summer. The latter is an annual
but it doesn't love our climate in
Ireland so it dies down in autumn
and really needs a greenhouse or
tunnel to grow enthusiastically,
even in summer.

✳ **PARSLEY** The multi-use herb
for both traditional and cutting-
edge dishes. Don't forget to chop
up stalks, they've got masses of
flavour, too.

✳ **THYME** A good variety of
common thyme definitely deserves
its place. It will even grow happily in
a large pot or bucket on a balcony.

✳ **ROSEMARY** Another multi-use
herb, it's a small shrub that can be
snipped throughout the year to add
to pasta sauces, stews or bread.

The purply-blue flowers make a
pretty garnish in late spring and
early summer and bees love them.

✳ **CHIVES** A few clumps of
chives are also invaluable. The
quintessential 'cut and come again'
herb that disappears underground
every winter to re-emerge in
early spring. Snip into and over
everything from omelettes and
frittatas to soups and stews.

✳ **MINT** This fresh-tasting herb
spreads like mad in the garden.
It's quite a 'thug', so plant it
somewhere you don't mind if it
romps away, or else in a bucket or
pot where its roots are curtailed.
I'm a big fan, so in my book you
can never have too much mint.
I use it in fistfuls in lemonades and
cocktails, salads and jellies. As with
many herbs, there are a number of
varieties. If you only have space for
one, choose spearmint.

✳ **CORIANDER** Not surprisingly the
most widely used herb in the world
because every scrap is edible. Use
the roots in Thai curry pastes, the
stalks are also full of flavour, as
are the fresh leaves. Sprinkle the
pretty white flowers over salads,
the green seeds have a unique and
thrilling flavour and add a burst of
excitement to many plates. When
they dry, hey presto, it's coriander
spice. Unlike the other herbs,
coriander is an annual and it runs
to seed quickly, so plant small
quantities in succession every few
weeks in summer.

ESSENTIAL KITCHEN EQUIPMENT

✱ **1 SET OF KNIVES** Buy the best you can afford – 1 chopping knife (cook's or chef's knife); 1 filleting knife; 1 vegetable or fruit paring knife; 1 serrated vegetable or fruit knife; 1 carving knife and 1 carving fork; 1 large and 1 small palette knife; 1 oyster knife (may seem not essential but you'll find that it's totally essential for the time you want to open oysters)

✱ **TOOLS** An accurate set of scales; 1 swivel-top peeler; 1 sharpening steel; 1 melon baller (not essential but handy); 1 zester (not essential but handy); 1 skewer; 1 stainless-steel grater; 2 sieves (1 tin or stainless steel, 1 plastic); 1 bottle opener; 1 corkscrew; 1 perforated spoon; 4 wooden spoons (2 large, 1 small, 1 straight-ended to get into corners of pans); 2 plastic spatulas (1 large, 1 small); 2 whisks (1 coil, 1 balloon); 2 fish slices (1 plastic, 1 tin); 1 bendy tin spatula (not essential but brilliant); 2 flat pastry brushes; 1 piping bag and set of nozzles (not essential but handy); 1 potato masher; 1 ladle; 1 rolling pin; 1 pepper mill; 1 salt crock (not essential but handy); 1 thermometer (not essential but handy to take the guesswork out of cooking time); mouli légumes – it may sit at the back of a cupboard for months but when you need it, nothing else with do.

✱ **MEASURING SPOONS**
1 teaspoon (5ml); 1 dessertspoon (10ml); 1 tablespoon (15ml); 1 x 225ml (8fl oz) cup
I measure with ordinary spoons that most people have in their kitchen drawers. Unless otherwise stated, I measure in rounded spoonfuls – a rounded spoonful has exactly the same amount on top as underneath. A heaped teaspoon has as much of the ingredients as the spoon will hold. A level teaspoon is just that and is the equivalent of a half-rounded teaspoon. If you are using standard measuring spoons, always use level measurements. My rounded measurements are the exact equivalent of a level measuring spoon. Also note that my tablespoon is the equivalent of 4 teaspoons whereas a standard measuring spoon holds just 3 teaspoons.

✱ **BOARDS** 1–2 heavy, hardwood timber chopping boards, at least 4cm (1½in) thick.
Mark the boards so that you know which surface to use. On the first board, mark one side for raw meat and the other side for onions. On the second board, mark one side for cooked food and the other side for fruit. If you have just one chopping board, mark one side R for raw and O for onion and garlic, then the other side C for cooked food and F for fruit.

✱ **SAUCEPANS** 1 large saucepan and lid (27 x 13cm/10 x 5in); 1 medium saucepan and lid (20 x 9cm/8 x 3½in); 1 small saucepan and lid; 1 high-sided sauté pan (20 x 9cm/8 x 3½in); 1 low-sided sauté pan (20 x 5.5cm/8 x 2in); 1 small saucepan (for boiling eggs, not essential but handy); 1 round/oval casserole with lid; 1 small round/oval casserole with lid; 1 non-stick frying pan (25cm/10in); 1 iron pan; 1 griddle pan
Buy the best heavy, stainless-steel saucepans you can afford. Some have a 50-year guarantee and you will be able to pass them on to your grandchildren. They don't burn or stick and do wonders for your cooking and your temper!

✱ **TINS** 1 or 2 quiche tins with removable bases (18cm/7in and 23cm/9in); 1 tart tin (size to fit requirements); 1 Swiss roll tin (25.5 x 38cm/10 x 15in); 2 x round cake tins (18cm/7in); 1 cupcake and/or muffin tin

✱ **BOWLS** 1 wide mixing bowl; 1 set of 5 stainless-steel mixing bowls, graded sizes; 1 set of 3 Pyrex bowls, graded sizes; 3–4 plastic bowls; 1 Pyrex plate for tarts (not essential but handy); 1 pie dish (1.2 litre/2 pints); 2 Pyrex measuring jugs; mais-gras for degreasing stock and gravy.

✳ MACHINES 1 food processor; 1 deep-fat fryer; 1 food mixer and/or handheld mixer; 1 juicer (electric if possible for large quantities); 1 liquidizer; 1 coffee grinder; 1 spice grinder; 1 slow cooker or Instant Pot.

✳ MISCELLANEOUS freezer bags and containers, Sharpie and labels; plastic containers for freezer; glass jars and lids; silicone muffin cases; baking parchment and or silicone baking sheets.

A pasta rolling machine and a dishwasher are also great if possible. My Nobel Peace Prize goes to the person who invented the dishwasher...!

USE-BY, SELL-BY & BEST BEFORE DATES

There seems to be constant confusion about these dates so I thought it would be helpful to include the definitions – it's worth remembering that ALL are conservative. Better still, learn the almost forgotten skill of using your senses to judge: look, smell, taste...

USE-BY DATE

This label is aimed at consumers as a directive of the date by which the product should be eaten; mostly because of quality, not because the item will necessarily make you sick if eaten after the use-by date. However, after the use-by date, product quality is likely to decrease much faster and safety could be reduced.

SELL-BY DATE

This label is aimed at retailers, to inform them of the date by which the product should be sold or removed from the shelf. This does not mean that the product is unsafe to consume after the date. Typically one-third of a product's shelf-life remains after the sell-by date for the consumer to use at home.

BEST BEFORE DATE

This is about quality, not safety. When the date is passed, it doesn't mean that the food will be harmful, but it might begin to lose its flavour and texture.

EVERYDAY STAPLES

A CLASSIC FRENCH OMELETTE

A simple French omelette takes 30 seconds to make or 45 seconds if you're adding a filling. Here at the Ballymaloe Cookery School, the students never believe me when I tell them this, they have their watches primed ready to catch me out! In no time they are turning out tender, golden 30-second omelettes themselves. The secret is to have the pan hot enough and to use clarified butter if at all possible. Ordinary butter will burn if your pan is as hot as it ought to be. It's also important to use the right-sized pan, otherwise the omelette will be too thick or thin and consequently overcooked or undercooked, so use the pan size specified below for a two-egg omelette. Your first omelette may not be a joy to behold but persevere – practice makes perfect!. You'll be an omelette whizz in no time, never stuck for a yummy meal.

SERVES 1 Ⓥ

2 fresh organic, free-range eggs
2 teaspoons whole milk
  or water
1 tablespoon clarified butter
  (see opposite) or
  1 tablespoon olive oil
filling of your choice (see
  opposite – optional)
sea salt and freshly ground
  black pepper

ADD EGGS, MILK, SALT & PEPPER

WHISK LIGHTLY

ADD CLARIFIED BUTTER OR OLIVE OIL

ONCE SIZZLING, ADD THE EGG. IT WILL START TO COOK IMMEDIATELY

PULL THE EDGES OF THE OMELETTE INTO THE CENTRE. TILT PAN SO UNCOOKED EGG RUNS TO THE SIDES

CONTINUE UNTIL THE EGG IS COOKED BUT STILL SOFT & MOIST

IF YOU ARE ADDING A FILLING, NOW IS THE TIME

FLIP THE EDGE NEAR THE HANDLE OVER THE FILLING. CHANGE YOUR GRIP ON THE HANDLE & FLIP AGAIN

...FINALLY FLIP/ROLL/SLIDE ON TO YOUR PLATE

Line up all your ingredients – this all happens so fast, there won't be time to go searching for something once you start. Warm a serving plate in a low oven.

Meanwhile, heat a 23cm (9in) omelette pan, preferably non-stick, over a high heat. Have your chosen filling and a spoon ready beside the cooker, heated if necessary.

Whisk the eggs with the milk or water in a bowl until thoroughly mixed but not too fluffy. Season with salt and pepper.

Put the warm serving plate beside the cooker/hob because you won't have time to go looking for it while the omelette is cooking.

Add the clarified butter or olive oil to the hot pan. As soon as it sizzles, pour in the egg mixture. Tilt from side to side to cover the base of the pan. It will start to cook immediately, so quickly pull the edges of the omelette towards the centre with a metal or plastic spatula, tilting the pan backwards and forwards then up and down for another few seconds so that the uncooked egg runs to the sides. Continue until most of the egg is set and will not run any more. The centre should still be soft and moist – don't worry, it will be perfectly cooked by the time it gets to the table. If you are using a filling, spoon the hot mixture in a line across the centre of the omelette, horizontal to the pan handle.

To fold the omelette: flip the omelette edge nearest the handle of the pan over the line of filling, towards the centre. Then change your grip of the handle so you are holding it from underneath, this will make it more comfortable for you to hold the pan almost upright so the omelette can roll towards the bottom of the pan. Half-roll and half-slide the omelette on to the plate so that it lands folded into three. Serve immediately with a salad of organic leaves (page 32) and a glass of something delicious.

TOP TIP ✱ For a delicious school or office lunch, slide the omelette into a toasted baguette. Add some leaves, maybe a tomato salad (page 34) and some relish.

FILLINGS

✱ **Mushroom à la crème** (page 28) Use 2–3 tablespoons as a filling.

✱ **Cheese & fresh herbs** Use 2 tablespoons of grated cheese and approx. 2 teaspoons of chopped flat-leaf parsley, tarragon, chives or thyme as a filling.

✱ **Smoked mackerel or smoked salmon & chives** Use 50–75g (2–3oz) diced or flaked fish and 1 teaspoon of chopped chives as a filling.

✱ **Piperonata or Tomato fondue** (pages 26 and 27) Use 2–3 tablespoons of hot tomato sauce as a filling, plus 1 sliced chilli or a pinch of chilli flakes, if you wish.

✱ **Crispy chorizo & parsley** Use 25g (1oz) crispy chorizo and 2 teaspoons of chopped flat-leaf parsley as a filling.

DARINA'S BASICS
CLARIFIED BUTTER ⓥ

Melt 225g (8oz) butter gently in a saucepan on the hob or in a Pyrex jug in the oven at 150°C/300°F/gas mark 2. Leave it to stand for a few minutes, then with a spoon, scrape the crusty white layer of salt particles off the top of the melted butter. Underneath this crust there is clear liquid butter which is called clarified butter. The milky liquid at the bottom can be discarded or used in a béchamel sauce (page 60). Clarified butter is excellent for cooking because it can withstand a higher temperature when the salt and milk particles are removed. It will keep covered in the fridge for several weeks.

BALLYMALOE BASIC RISOTTO

Everyone needs to be able to whip up a risotto, comfort food at its best and a base for so many good things, from crispy pork lardons or kale to foraged nettles.

SERVES 6

1–1.3 litres (1¾–2¼ pints) chicken or vegetable stock (page 30)
50g (2oz) butter
2 tablespoons extra virgin olive oil
1 onion, finely chopped
400g (14oz) risotto rice, such as arborio, carnaroli, or Vialone Nano
50g (2oz) freshly grated Parmesan cheese or a mixture of Parmesan and Pecorino
sea salt

First bring the stock to the boil, reduce the heat and keep it at a gentle simmer. Melt half the butter in a heavy-bottomed saucepan with the oil, add the onion, cover and sweat over a gentle heat for 4–5 minutes until soft but not coloured. Add the rice and stir until well coated. Cook for a minute or so and then add 150ml (5fl oz) of the simmering stock, stir continuously, and as soon as the liquid is absorbed add another 150ml (5fl oz) of stock. Continue to cook, stirring constantly. The heat should be brisk, but on the other hand if it's too hot the rice will be soft outside but still chewy inside. If it's too slow, the rice will be gluey. It's difficult to know which is worse, so the trick is to regulate the heat so that the rice bubbles continuously. The risotto should take 25–30 minutes to cook.

After about 20 minutes, add the stock about 4 tablespoons at a time. I use a small ladle. Watch it very carefully from there on. The risotto is done when the rice is cooked but is still ever so slightly al dente. It should be soft and creamy and quite loose, rather than thick. The moment you are happy with the texture, stir in the remaining butter and Parmesan, taste and add more salt if necessary. Serve immediately on hot plates.

Alternatively, you can pre-cook the rice for finishing later. After about 10 minutes of cooking, taste a grain or two between your teeth. It should be firm, slightly gritty, definitely undercooked but not completely raw. Remove the risotto from the saucepan and spread it out on a flat dish to cool as quickly as possible. The rice can be reheated later with some of the remaining stock and the cooking and finishing of the risotto can be completed.

GOOD THINGS WITH RISOTTO

✱ **Prawn risotto** Add 110–175g (4–6oz) cooked and peeled prawns to the risotto just before the end of cooking. 1–2 tablespoons of freshly chopped dill is also a delicious addition. If possible, use shrimp or fish stock but light chicken stock works too. The Italians are adamant that no cheese should be served with fish but I love it, so you decide…

✱ **Kale risotto** Destalk 450g (1lb) curly or red Russian kale, or cavolo nero. Bring 3.4 litres (6 pints) of water to the boil in a large saucepan with 3 teaspoons of salt. Add the kale leaves and boil, uncovered, over a high heat until tender; this can vary from 5–10 minutes depending on the weather and the age of the kale. Drain well, chop and stir into the risotto about 5 minutes before the end of cooking. Season to taste and serve sprinkled with grated Parmesan cheese.

✱ **Nettle & sorrel risotto** Blanch and refresh 110g (4oz) nettles, drain and season well. Add to the risotto with 50g (2oz) sorrel. Add another knob of butter if necessary and lots of Parmesan.

✱ **Wild garlic risotto** Finely chop approx. 110g (4oz) wild garlic leaves and add to the risotto 3–4 minutes before the end of cooking. Scatter with wild garlic flowers, if available, and serve immediately.

✱ Mushroom risotto Add 225–350g (8–12oz) sliced and sautéed mushrooms before the end of cooking.

✱ Risi e bisi (Pea & broad bean risotto) Blanch 500g (18oz) fresh young peas or young broad beans in boiling salted water, then drain. Season with lots of freshly ground black pepper and add 45g (1½oz) butter. Put half of this into a food processor and pulse. Return to the whole peas or beans. Cook 200g (7oz) chopped onions in 40g (1½oz) butter, add 300g (10½oz) risotto rice and 1.75 litres (3 pints) chicken or vegetable stock and cook as above. After 15 minutes, add the peas and 3 tablespoons of chopped flat-leaf parsley to the risotto and continue to cook for about 5 minutes until the rice is al dente. Stir in 40g (1½oz) butter, 100g (3½oz) freshly grated Parmesan cheese and season to taste. Serve with a little more Parmesan sprinkled over the top.

✱ Arancini Arancini are crispy rice balls usually made from leftover risotto (spread the risotto over a baking tray to cool). Flavour the risotto as desired – arancini can be plain or flavoured with a myriad of tasty additions, including ragù, wild mushrooms, mozzarella, aubergines, wild fennel, shellfish or pistachios. To make, scoop up a fistful of cold risotto, shape into a round, slightly oval or conical shape. Dip in white breadcrumbs and deep-fry in hot olive oil for 4–5 minutes until crisp. Drain on kitchen paper and serve hot.

SWEAT THE CHOPPED ONION IN THE BUTTER & OIL

ADD THE RICE & STIR UNTIL WELL COATED

ADD A LADLEFUL OF STOCK AT A TIME

THE RISOTTO SHOULD BE SOFT, CREAMY & QUITE LOOSE

DELICIOUS ROAST CHICKEN

Who doesn't love a classic roast chicken with lots of gravy? It's a forgotten flavour for many, partly because unless you have access to a really good bird, the smell and flavour will be quite different to your comforting childhood memories. People often feel that making stuffing is too much of a bother, but if you keep some breadcrumbs in the freezer it can literally be made in minutes. The best place for the stuffing is inside the chicken, where it absorbs lots of delicious juices as it cooks. Be careful not to overfill the bird, otherwise the heat may not penetrate fully. This is particularly important if you are using an intensively reared chicken, which may be infected with salmonella and/or campylobacter.

SERVES 6 OR MORE

1.5–2.3kg (3½–5lb) free-range chicken, preferably organic or at least free-range

600–900ml (1–1½ pints) stock from giblets or chicken stock (see below)

FOR THE STOCK (OPTIONAL)

giblets (keep the liver for a chicken liver pâté), and wishbone

1 carrot, thickly sliced

1 onion, thickly sliced

1 celery stick, thickly sliced

a few parsley stalks and a sprig of thyme

FOR THE STUFFING

75g (3oz) chopped onion

45g (1½oz) butter, plus extra for greasing

75–100g (3–3½oz) soft, fresh white breadcrumbs

2 tablespoons finely chopped fresh herbs, such as flat-leaf parsley, thyme, chives and annual marjoram

sea salt and freshly ground black pepper

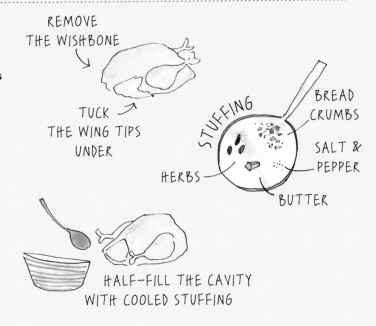

REMOVE THE WISHBONE

TUCK THE WING TIPS UNDER

STUFFING

BREAD CRUMBS

SALT & PEPPER

HERBS

BUTTER

HALF-FILL THE CAVITY WITH COOLED STUFFING

COOK FOR 20 MINUTES PER 450g (1lb) PLUS 20 MINUTES

Remove the wishbone from the neck end of the chicken by lifting back the loose neck, skin and cutting around the wishbone with a small knife – tug to remove. This isn't essential, but it does make carving much easier. Tuck the wing tips underneath the chicken to make a neat shape. Put the wishbone, giblets, carrot, onions, celery and herbs into a saucepan. Cover with cold water, bring to the boil, skim off any foam and simmer gently while the chicken is roasting. This is the base of the gravy.

To make the stuffing, sweat the onion gently in the butter for about 10 minutes until soft, then stir in the breadcrumbs, herbs and a little salt and pepper to taste. Allow it to get quite cold unless you are going to cook the chicken immediately. Season the chicken cavity with salt and pepper and half-fill with stuffing. Season the breast and legs, smear with a little soft butter or a drizzle of extra virgin olive oil.

Preheat the oven to 180°C/350°F/gas mark 4. Weigh the chicken and cook for 20 minutes per 450g (1lb), plus 20 minutes. Cook on the middle shelf in the oven. Baste a couple of times during the cooking with the buttery juices. The chicken is done when the juices are running clear. To test, prick the thickest part at the base of the thigh, hold a spoon underneath to collect the liquid, examine the juices – they should be clear. Remove the chicken to a carving dish, keep it warm and leave to rest while you make the gravy.

To make the gravy, tilt the roasting tin to one corner, spoon off the surplus fat and return the roasting tin to the stove. De-glaze the tin juices with the fat-free stock from the giblets and bones (you will need 600–900ml/1–1½ pints) depending on the size of the chicken. Using a whisk, stir and scrape well to dissolve the caramelized meat juices in the roasting tin. Boil it well, season and thicken with a little roux (page 60) if you like (the gravy should not be too thick). Season to taste and serve in a hot gravy boat. If possible, serve the chicken on a nice carving dish surrounded by crispy roast potatoes and some sprigs of flat-leaf parsley, then arm yourself with a sharp knife and bring it to the table.

Carve into six portions or more, depending on the size of the chicken. Each portion should have some brown and white meat and bone and some stuffing. First, carve off the leg. Separate the drumstick from the thigh, and if the leg is big, the thigh can be divided into two portions, one piece with a bone and one without. Put on a hot serving dish. Carve off a generous piece of white meat with the wing attached and serve with the piece of thigh with no bone to make one portion. Then carve the remaining white meat into slices; put some with the drumstick and some with the thigh piece with a bone to make two more portions. Repeat on the other side. Serve with gravy and bread sauce, if you wish.

VARIATIONS

* **Herb butter** Add 1–2 tablespoons of chopped tarragon, thyme or rosemary to the butter. Lift the skin off the breast and smear the butter directly on to the flesh before cooking.

* **Sans stuffing** Omit the stuffing. Season the interior of the chicken with salt and pepper and insert a sprig or two of tarragon, rosemary or thyme. Or season the interior, then prick a lemon (preferably organic) in a few places and insert into the cavity while the chicken is roasting.

* **Masala roast chicken** Add a mixture of freshly ground spices, such as 1–2 tablespoons of smoked paprika or harissa, 1 teaspoon of cumin, 1 teaspoon of coriander to 4 tablespoons of olive oil and spread over the chicken before roasting.

* **Casserole roast chicken** Insert a sprig of tarragon in the cavity. Slather the breast and legs with tarragon butter. Cover and cook the casserole in a moderate oven for 1¼–1½ hours. Degrease, add 150ml (5fl oz) cream and 150ml (5fl oz) stock to the juices, thicken with a little roux. Serve with the tarragon sauce.

A SIMPLE SOUP

This technique works for any number of root and leafy vegetables as well as foraged greens. It's really useful to be able to whip up a soup in minutes with whatever you can find in your fridge or pantry. The onion and potatoes form the base – the melted onion adds natural sweetness and the potato provides body. You can use just a single vegetable, such as carrots, or a mixture, such as carrot, parsnip and celeriac or swede, or pea, bean and courgette, or spinach, watercress and lettuce. More than half the soups we make at Ballymaloe are made on this simple formula – 1:1:3:5. Use the same measure for each ingredient – it could be a cup, mug, jam jar or whatever is handy. Soups made with stock will have more flavour than those made with water, but if the vegetables are fresh, the soup will still be tasty. You can also add fresh herbs or spices to perk it up. It's fun to experiment, the flavour will be different each time and the end result will be a surprise but always delicious.

SERVES 6 **V** if using vegetable stock or water

50g (2oz) butter or 3 tablespoons olive oil or a mixture
1 part chopped onions
1 part chopped potatoes
approx. 2 tablespoons fresh herbs and/or
  1–3 teaspoons spices (optional)
3 parts any vegetable of your choice, or a mixture
5 parts hot chicken or vegetable stock (page 30) or
  water, or a mixture of stock and milk
sea salt and freshly ground black pepper

Melt the butter in a heavy-bottomed saucepan. When it foams, add the onions and potatoes (and herbs or spices, if using) and turn them until well coated with butter. Sprinkle with salt and pepper. Cover and sweat over a gentle heat for 10 minutes until the onions are soft but not coloured. Add the vegetables and boiling stock. Cook until just tender. Liquidize to a smooth purée or serve as a chunky soup. Do not overcook or the vegetables will lose their flavour. Taste and adjust the seasoning if necessary.

CHOP ONIONS, POTATOES & ANOTHER VEGETABLE OF YOUR CHOICE

MELT THE BUTTER, ADD ONIONS & POTATOES & SWEAT FOR 10 MINUTES

ADD THE THIRD VEGETABLE & HOT STOCK. SEASON & COOK UNTIL THE VEGETABLES ARE TENDER.

LIQUIDIZE & CHECK SEASONING. EAT WITH HUGE PRIDE!

PESTO

Pesto, the famous Ligurian basil sauce, is best made with summer basil and Italian pine nuts. The price of pine nuts has skyrocketed in recent years so I now use cashews instead, which work brilliantly. Home-peeled almonds are also a good alternative. Homemade pesto takes minutes to make and tastes a million times better than most of what you can buy. To avoid mould growing, clean the top of the jar every time you take some out and cover the surface of the pesto with a layer of olive oil to exclude the air. That way you should be able to use every scrap. I make a wide variety of pestos throughout the year depending on the season – enjoy experimenting with the variations listed opposite or swap the basil leaves for watercress in the recipe below.

MAKES APPROX. 2 X 200ML (7FL OZ) JARS

110g (4oz) fresh basil leaves or watercress
175–225ml (6–8fl oz) extra virgin olive oil
25g (1oz) cashews or fresh pine nuts (taste when you buy to make sure they are not rancid), chopped
2 large garlic cloves, crushed
50g (2oz) finely grated Parmesan cheese (Parmigiano Reggiano is best)
sea salt, to taste

Whizz the basil (or watercress) with the olive oil, chopped cashews or pine nuts and garlic in a food processor or pound in a pestle and mortar. Remove to a bowl and fold in the Parmesan cheese. Season to taste.

Pesto keeps for weeks, covered with a layer of olive oil in a jar in the fridge. It also freezes well but for best results don't add the grated Parmesan until it has defrosted. Freeze in small jars or containers for convenience.

VARIATIONS

* **Parsley pesto** (Makes 2 x 150ml/ 5fl oz jars) – Finely chop 35g (1¼oz) cashews. Put into a food processor with 50g (2oz) flat-leaf parsley leaves and 2 garlic cloves and whizz for a second or two. Gradually add 200ml (7fl oz) extra virgin olive oil. Add 50g (2oz) freshly grated Parmesan cheese, whizz for another couple of seconds. Season to taste.

* **Kale pesto** (Makes 4 x 150ml/5fl oz jars) Strip 450g (1lb) curly kale from the stalks and clean well. If you prefer a mellower flavour, blanch the kale in boiling salted water for 3–4 minutes, refresh and drain well. Put into a food processor with 1 garlic clove, 2 teaspoons of sea salt, 50g (2oz) freshly grated Parmesan cheese and 325–350ml (11–12fl oz) extra virgin olive oil and whizz to a thick paste. Stored in a covered jar in the fridge for several days. Serve on crostini or drizzle over soups and stews.

* **Wild garlic pesto** Wash 110g (4oz) wild garlic leaves, spin and destalk. Whizz in a food processor with 50g (2oz) chopped cashews, 2 garlic cloves, ¼ teaspoon of salt and 350–450ml (12–16fl oz) olive oil. Remove to a bowl and fold in 80g (3oz) freshly grated Parmesan cheese. Season to taste with sugar if necessary.

IRISH WHITE SODA BREAD & SCONES

Soda bread takes only a few minutes to make and 30–40 minutes to bake. I have so much fun experimenting – you can make a loaf or scones, or spread the dough out on a 31 x 23 x 5cm (12½ x 9 x 2in) roasting tin, top it with tomato sauce and pepperoni and, hey presto, you've got a soda bread pizza. There's really no end to the possibilities, both sweet and savoury. You can also make Brown Soda Bread (see Variations). If you accidentally make the dough too wet, bake in a tin rather than a traditional round loaf. Soda breads are best eaten on the day they are made. Shop-bought buttermilk is usually low fat but if you have access to rich, thick buttermilk, there is no need to add butter or extra cream. Some people add 1 beaten egg for extra richness, reduce the buttermilk by 50ml (2fl oz).

MAKES 1 LOAF **V**

450g (1lb) plain flour, preferably unbleached
1 level teaspoon teaspoon salt
1 level teaspoon teaspoon bicarbonate of soda
approx. 350–400ml (12–14fl oz) buttermilk or sour milk to mix, depending on thickness of the milk

Preheat the oven to 230°C/450°F/gas mark 8.

Sift the dry ingredients into a large bowl. Make a well in the centre. Pour most of the buttermilk in at once. Using one hand, mix in the flour from the sides of the bowl, adding more milk if necessary. The dough should be softish, not too wet and sticky. When it all comes together, turn it out on to a well-floured worktop.

Wash and dry your hands. Tidy it up and flip over gently. Pat the dough into a disc about 4cm (1½in) thick, then cut a cross in it to let the fairies out! Let the cuts go over the sides of the bread to make sure of this. Bake for 15 minutes, then reduce the oven temperature to 200°C/400°F/gas mark 6 for 30 minutes or until cooked. If you are in doubt, tap the bottom of the bread: if it is cooked it will sound hollow.

VARIATIONS

* **Brown soda bread** Make in the same way as the white bread using 225g (8oz) wholemeal flour (preferably stoneground), 225g (8oz) plain flour, 1 teaspoon salt, 1 level teaspoon of bicarbonate of soda, 12–25g (¼–1oz) butter or 2 tablespoons of fresh or soured cream, 400–425ml (14–15fl oz) buttermilk or sour milk. If you prefer a lighter bread, use 450g (1lb) plain flour and 150g (5oz) wholemeal flour. Bake for 10 minutes, then reduce the oven temperature to 200°C/400°F/gas mark 6 and cook for a further 30 minutes. Turn the bread upside down on the baking tray and continue to cook for 5–10 minutes. The bread will sound hollow when tapped on both sides. Cool on a wire rack, wrapped in a clean tea towel while hot, if you prefer a softer crust. You can also add 1 tablespoon of fine oatmeal, bran or wheatgerm, 1 egg and 12g (¼oz) butter to the dough to make a richer soda bread.

* **Cheddar cheese soda bread** Egg wash the surface of the bread, then scatter with 110g (4oz) grated mature Cheddar cheese. Mark into 6–8 wedges with a knife and bake as above.

* **White soda scones** Make the dough as in the main recipe but flatten it into a round 2.5cm (1in) deep. Cut into 10–12 scones. Dip in 25g (1oz) oatmeal, kibbled wheat or a selection of seeds, such as sesame, poppy or pumpkin. Cook for about 20 minutes at 230°C/450°F/gas mark 8.

* **White soda bread with herbs** Add 2 tablespoons of freshly chopped herbs, such as rosemary, lovage, thyme, chives, flat-leaf parsley or lemon balm, to the dry ingredients and continue as in the main recipe, shaping into a loaf or scones.

* **Cheddar cheese scones or herb & cheese scones** Make the White Soda bread or herb dough (above). Stamp into scones, brush the top of each one with beaten egg and then dip into 110g (4oz) grated Cheddar cheese. Bake as for soda scones, or use to cover the top of a casserole or stew.

* **Rosemary & olive scones** Add 1½ tablespoons of chopped rosemary and 2 tablespoons of roughly chopped stoned black olives to the dry ingredients and proceed as in the main recipe.

* **Rosemary & sun-dried tomato bread or scones** Add 1–2 tablespoons of chopped rosemary, 2 tablespoons of chopped sun-dried tomatoes to the flour and continue as in the main recipe. Form into a loaf or scones.

* **Bacon or chorizo scones** Add 175g (6oz) diced sautéed bacon or 110g (4oz) chorizo to the flour and continue as in the main recipe.

* **Olive scones** Make a white soda bread dough with or without herbs. Flatten into a 2.5cm (1in) deep square. Dot the top with whole, stoned, olives and a sprig of thyme or rosemary, if you wish. Brush generously with olive oil, sprinkle with sea salt, cut into square scones and bake as above.

* **Rosemary & raisin soda bread** Add 75g (3oz) raisins and 2 tablespoons of chopped rosemary to the dough and proceed as in the main recipe.

* **Curry & sultana bread** Add 1–2 teaspoons of curry powder and 75g (3oz) sultanas to the dough and proceed as in the main recipe.

* **American emigrants' soda bread** Add 75g (3oz) sultanas and 1–2 teaspoons of caraway seeds, 1 tablespoon of sugar and 1 beaten egg to the dough and reduce the buttermilk by 50ml (2fl oz). Bake at 230°C/450°F/gas mark 8 for 5 minutes, then reduce the oven temperature to 180°C/350°F/gas mark 4 and bake for 30–35 minutes.

* **Seeded tear & share scones** Make the dough as in the main recipe. Brush a 23cm (9in) round tin with sunflower oil. Pat the dough into a round, about 4cm (1½in) deep, and cut a cross in the top to divide into eight pieces. Put into the tin and brush the top of the scones with a selection of sesame, poppy, pumpkin and sunflower seeds. Bake as in the main recipe. Remove from the tin and cool on a wire rack. The bread can then be torn apart and shared!

BALLYMALOE BROWN YEAST BREAD

This recipe is a brilliant introduction to yeast bread making. There is no kneading and only one rising. It takes about 1½ hours from start to finish but the mixing takes less than 5 minutes, the rest is rising and baking time. Delicious on the day it's made, it keeps brilliantly for several days and is good toasted for up to a week.

Have the ingredients and equipment at blood heat. You can use white or brown sugar, honey, or golden syrup instead of the treacle or molasses. Each will give a slightly different flavour to the bread. Different brands of flour produce breads of different texture and flavour. The amount of moisture in the flour varies according to atmospheric conditions. The quantity of water should be altered accordingly. You can also use 400g (14oz) strong wholemeal flour and 50g (2oz) rye flour or just 450g (1lb) strong wholemeal flour. Dried yeast can be used but use half the weight given for fresh yeast. Allow longer to rise for fast-action yeast and follow the packet instructions.

MAKES 1 LOAF Ve

400g (14oz) strong wholemeal bread flour
50g (2oz) strong white bread flour
1 teaspoon salt
1 teaspoon black treacle or molasses
425ml (15fl oz) water at blood heat
20–30g (¾–1oz) non-GM yeast or 7g sachet fast-action yeast
good-quality sunflower oil, for greasing
1 dessertspoon sesame seeds (optional)

Mix both flours with the salt in a wide bowl. In a small bowl or Pyrex jug, mix the treacle with 150ml (5fl oz) of the water and crumble in the yeast – do not stir. Leave in a warm place for a few minutes to allow the yeast to start to work. After about 3–5 minutes it will have a creamy and slightly frothy top. Stir and pour it, with the remaining water, into the dry ingredients to make a loose dough, too wet to knead. Cover the bowl and leave to sit for 4–5 minutes (depending on room temperature). Preheat the oven to 230°C/450°F/gas mark 8.

Brush a 13 x 20cm (5 x 8in) loaf tin with oil. Scoop the dough into the tin. Sprinkle with sesame seeds, if you like. Put the tin in a warm place – close to the cooker or near a radiator both work well. Cover with a tea towel to prevent a skin from forming. After 10–15 minutes, just as the dough comes to the top of the tin, uncover and bake for 20 minutes, then reduce the temperature to 200°C/400°F/gas mark 6 and bake for 40–50 minutes or until it is nicely browned and sounds hollow when tapped. I usually remove the loaf from the tin about 10 minutes before the end of cooking and return it to the oven to crisp all over, but if you like a softer crust there's no need to do this. Cool on a wire rack.

VARIATION

✱ Cheat's no-fuss white yeast bread
Make a white version with 450g (1lb) strong white bread flour, 1 teaspoon of salt, 1 teaspoon of honey, 300ml (10fl oz) tepid water, 20–25g (¾–1oz) fresh non-GM yeast or 7g sachet fast-action yeast and 1 dessertspoon of sesame seeds (optional). Leave the dough for 30 minutes to rise to the top of the tin, but bake in the same way.

BASIC SHORTCRUST PASTRY

This recipe makes a short, crisp, crumbly but not brittle pastry – use for savoury tarts, quiches and pies. To make a sweet version, follow the same recipe substituting 1 dessertspoon of caster or icing sugar for the salt.

MAKES ENOUGH PASTRY TO LINE A 23CM (9IN) FLAN RING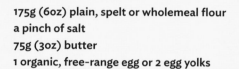

175g (6oz) plain, spelt or wholemeal flour
a pinch of salt
75g (3oz) butter
1 organic, free-range egg or 2 egg yolks

Sift the flour and salt into a large bowl. Cut the butter into cubes, and toss in the flour. Incorporating some air each time, with your thumb, rub the butter across your middle fingers over and over until the texture resembles coarse breadcrumbs, then stop. Keep everything as cool as possible; if the fat is allowed to melt, the finished pastry may be tough.

Whisk the egg or egg yolks and add some water. Using a fork to stir, add just enough of this liquid to bring the pastry together, then discard the fork and collect the dough into a ball with your hands, this way you can judge more accurately if you need a few more drops of liquid. Although rather damp pastry is easier to handle and roll out, the resulting crust can be tough and may well shrink out of shape as the water evaporates in the oven. Drier and more difficult-to-handle pastry will give a crisper, shorter crust.

Flatten into a round, wrap the pastry in clingfilm and leave to rest in the fridge for at least 15 minutes. This will make the pastry much less elastic and easier to roll. Use as needed.

VARIATION

✱ **Hot water crust pastry** (Makes enough for a 17.5cm/6¾in pie) Sift 350g (12oz) plain flour and a pinch of salt into a bowl and make a well in the centre. Put 175g (6oz) diced butter into a saucepan with 110ml (4fl oz) water and bring to the boil. Pour the liquid into the flour all at once and mix together quickly with a wooden spoon; beat until smooth. The pastry will be too soft to handle, but as soon as it cools use it as you wish.

PIZZA DOUGH

This recipe is so quick and easy as using fast-action yeast does away with the first rising.

MAKES 8 X 25CM (10IN) PIZZAS Ⓥ

680g (1lb 8oz) strong white bread flour or 600g (1lb 5oz) strong white bread flour and 110g (4oz) rye flour
2 level teaspoons salt
15g (½oz) granulated sugar
50g (2oz) butter
7g sachet fast-action yeast
2–4 tablespoons olive oil, plus extra for brushing
450–500ml (16–18fl oz) lukewarm water, plus extra if needed

Sift the flours into a large mixing bowl. Add the salt and sugar. Rub in the butter, add the yeast and mix thoroughly. Make a well in the centre, add the oil and most of the lukewarm water. Mix to a loose dough. Add more water or flour if needed. Turn the dough on to a lightly floured worktop, cover and leave to relax for about 5 minutes.

Knead the dough for 10 minutes or until smooth and springy. You can also do this in a mixer fitted with the dough hook for 5 minutes. Cover with a tea towel and leave the dough to relax for about 10 minutes.

Shape the dough into 8 balls weighing about 150g (5oz) each. Lightly brush with olive oil. If you have time, put into a plastic bag and chill as they are easier to handle when cold but can be used immediately.

On a well-floured worktop, roll each ball into a 25cm (10in) disc. Top with your chosen toppings and bake at 250°C/475°F/gas mark 9 for 10–12 minutes.

TOMATO SAUCE

A good tomato sauce is invaluable to have in the fridge or freezer as a standby and gives you pasta sauce in seconds. Canned tomatoes vary dramatically in quality – buy the best you can source or it is impossible to get a good result.

MAKES 475ML (17FL OZ) Ⓥ

25g (1oz) butter
2 tablespoons extra virgin olive oil
1–4 garlic cloves, depending on taste, chopped
1 medium onion, finely chopped
900g (2lb) very ripe tomatoes, peeled and chopped, or 2 x 400g (14oz) cans Italian chopped tomatoes
honey, to sweeten (optional)
sea salt, freshly ground black pepper and sugar

Melt the butter, add the olive oil and toss in the garlic. Cook for 1–2 minutes or until pale golden, then add the onion and cook for a minute or two before adding the chopped tomatoes and juice. Season with salt, pepper and sugar. Cook for 15–20 minutes if you want a fresh-tasting sauce, or slowly – for up to 1 hour – if you prefer it more concentrated. Purée through a mouli légumes or sieve. Season to taste. Add a little sugar or honey if necessary, particularly if using canned tomatoes.

Tomato sauce will keep in the fridge for about a week and in the freezer for several months.

VARIATIONS

✱ **Tomato & chilli sauce** Add 1–2 sliced chillies or ¼–1 teaspoon of chilli flakes with the tomatoes. For a quick Arrabbiata sauce, add 2–3 tablespoons of basil, marjoram, mint, rosemary or thyme – not traditional, but I love coriander too.

✱ **Tomato & ginger sauce** Add 1–2 teaspoons of grated ginger to the sweated onion and proceed as above. Serve with fish, chicken or halloumi.

✱ **Tomato & paprika sauce** Add 1–2 teaspoons of smoked paprika with the onion.

PIPERONATA

This is one of the indispensable trio of vegetable stews that I always reckon to have to hand. I use it not only as a vegetable side but also as a topping for pizzas (page 25), as a sauce for pasta, grilled fish or meat, or as a filling for omelettes (page 15) and pancakes.

SERVES 8–10 Ⓥe

2 tablespoons olive oil
1 garlic clove, crushed
225g (8oz) onion, sliced
2 red peppers, deseeded and cut into 2–2.5cm (¾–1in) pieces
2 green peppers, deseeded and cut into 2–2.5cm (¾–1in) pieces
6 large, very ripe tomatoes
a few fresh basil leaves (optional)
sea salt, freshly ground black pepper and sugar

Heat the olive oil in a casserole, add the garlic and cook for a few seconds, then add the onion, toss in the oil, cover and soften over a gentle heat for 5–6 minutes. Add the peppers to the onion and toss in the oil; replace the lid and continue to cook for 5–6 minutes.

Meanwhile, scald the tomatoes in boiling water for 10 seconds, pour off the water and peel immediately. Slice the tomatoes and add to the casserole, season with salt, pepper, sugar and a few fresh basil leaves, if available. Cook for 30 minutes until the vegetables are just soft.

Piperonata will keep in the fridge for 7–10 days and freezes brilliantly but is best eaten within 1–2 months.

TOMATO FONDUE

This is a culinary marvel that I can't survive without as it has a million uses; serve it as a vegetable side or a sauce for pasta, a filling for omelettes (page 15), a topping for pizza (page 25) or as a base for leftover meat, vegetables or fish. Always make more than you need and make sure to have some stashed in your freezer. Late-summer tomatoes have the best flavour and really ripe ones freeze brilliantly, just throw them into a box or freezer bag.

SERVES APPROX. 6 **Ve**
2 tablespoons extra virgin olive oil
110g (4oz) sliced onions
1 garlic clove, crushed
900g (2lb) very ripe tomatoes, peeled, in summer or 2 x 400g (14oz) best-quality cans plum tomatoes in winter
1 tablespoon chopped mint, thyme, parsley, lemon balm, marjoram or torn basil
a splash of balsamic vinegar (optional)
sea salt, freshly ground black pepper and sugar

Heat the oil in a stainless-steel sauté pan or casserole. Add the onions and garlic and toss until coated, cover and sweat over a gentle heat for about 10 minutes until soft but not coloured. It is vital that the onions are completely soft before the tomatoes are added. Chop the fresh or canned tomatoes and add to the onions along with their juice. Season with salt, pepper and sugar (canned tomatoes need lots of sugar because of their high acidity). Add the herbs of your choice. Cover and cook for 10–20 minutes or until the tomatoes soften. Cook fresh tomatoes for a shorter time to preserve their lively flavour. Uncover and reduce a little. A few drops of balsamic vinegar greatly enhances the flavour. Canned tomatoes need to be cooked for longer depending on whether you want to use the fondue as a vegetable, sauce or filling. Just reduce, uncovered, to the required consistency. It will keep in the fridge for 10–14 days or the freezer for 2–3 months.

TOMATO PURÉE

A brilliant way to preserve a glut of your own homegrown tomatoes or lots of very ripe tomatoes in late summer. We make gallons of tomato purée at the end of the season when the tomatoes are packed with flavour – it's brilliant to have in the freezer for tomato soup, stews and casseroles.

MAKES APPROX. 300ML (10FL OZ)
900g (2lb) very ripe tomatoes
1 small onion, chopped
1 teaspoon sugar
a good pinch of sea salt and a few twists of black pepper

Cut the tomatoes into quarters, put into a stainless-steel saucepan with the onion, sugar, salt and pepper. Cook over a gentle heat for 15–20 minutes until the tomatoes are soft (no water needed). Put through the fine blade of the mouli légumes or a nylon sieve. Leave to get cold, then refrigerate or freeze for 3–4 months but best used within 2–3 months.

VARIATIONS

✱ **Tomato & chilli fondue** Add 1–2 chopped fresh chillies to the onions when sweating.

✱ **Penne with tomato fondue** Toss 450g (1lb) cooked penne or spaghetti with Tomato & chilli fondue (above).

✱ **Tomato fondue with sausages** Add 1–2 sliced cabanossi to the tomato fondue 5 minutes before the end of cooking – great with pasta. A pack of chorizo, soppressata or 'nduja can also be added.

MUSHROOM À LA CRÈME

Another great convertible and a brilliant standby. I use
this creamy mushroom à la crème as a sauce for steak,
chicken, lamb or veal, on burgers or pasta, as a filling for
an omelette (page 15), a topping for pizza (page 25), a
base for a chicken and ham pie or to slather on toast. Flat
mushrooms or chestnut mushrooms have more flavour
than button mushrooms (include the sliced stalks).
Mushroom à la crème doesn't freeze particularly well but
does keep covered in the fridge for 4–5 days. I sometimes
add a teaspoon of grated ginger or a crushed clove of
garlic to the onions when sweating – delicious!

SERVES 4 Ⓥ

15–25g (½–1oz) butter
75g (3oz) onions, finely chopped
olive oil, for frying
225g (8oz) mushrooms, sliced
a squeeze of lemon juice
110ml (4fl oz) single cream
20–25g (¾–1oz) roux (page 60)
1 tablespoon chopped flat-leaf parsley
½ tablespoon chopped chives (optional)
sea salt and freshly ground black pepper

Melt the butter in a heavy saucepan until it foams. Add the onions,
cover and sweat over a gentle heat for 5–10 minutes or until quite
soft but not coloured.

Meanwhile, cook the sliced mushrooms in olive oil, in a hot frying
pan, for 4–5 minutes or until they are browning at the edges, in
batches if necessary. Season with salt, pepper and a tiny squeeze of
lemon juice. Add the mushrooms to the onions, then add the cream
and allow to bubble for a few minutes. Thicken with a little roux to
a light coating consistency. Season to taste and add the parsley and
chives, if using.

VARIATIONS

✱ **Mushroom à la crème
with marjoram** Stir through
1–2 tablespoons of chopped annual
marjoram instead of the parsley and
chives at the end of cooking.

✱ **Mushroom & ginger sauce**
Substitute 1 teaspoon of grated ginger
for the herbs and proceed as in the
main recipe.

✱ **Pasta with sautéed mushrooms,
extra virgin olive oil & marjoram**
Sweat the onions and mushrooms in
extra virgin olive oil instead of butter
(I use Capezzana). Add 2 tablespoons
of chopped marjoram instead of the
parsley and chives. Toss through 500g
(18oz) cooked pasta with lots of extra
virgin olive oil and a good sprinkling of
Parmesan.

SPICED AUBERGINES

This super versatile recipe is delicious with a dollop of labneh (page 113) or alongside pan-grilled lamb chops or roast pork with crackling.

SERVES 6 Ve

265ml (9¼fl oz) extra virgin olive oil

500g (18oz) aubergines, cut into 2cm- (¾in-) thick slices

2.5cm (1in) piece of fresh ginger, peeled and coarsely grated

6 large garlic cloves, crushed

6 tablespoons extra virgin olive oil

1 teaspoon fennel seeds

2 teaspoons cumin seeds

350g (12oz) very ripe tomatoes, peeled and finely chopped, or 400g (14oz) can chopped tomatoes

1 teaspoon sugar

1 tablespoon ground coriander

¼ teaspoon ground turmeric

⅓ teaspoon cayenne pepper

25–50g (1–2oz) raisins

sea salt

Heat 175ml (6fl oz) of the oil in a 25–30cm (10–12in) frying pan. When almost smoking, add a few aubergine slices and cook until golden and tender on both sides. Remove and drain on a wire rack over a baking sheet. Repeat with the remaining aubergines, adding more oil if necessary. Alternatively, brush with oil and cook in a hot griddle plan. Put the ginger, garlic and 50ml (2fl oz) water into a blender. Blend until fairly smooth.

Heat the remaining 6 tablespoons of oil in a frying pan. When hot, add the fennel and cumin seeds (be careful not to let them burn). Stir for just a few seconds, then add the tomatoes and sugar, plus the ginger-garlic mixture, ground spices and a generous pinch of salt. Simmer for 5–6 minutes, stirring occasionally, until the spice mixture thickens slightly. Add the fried aubergines and raisins and coat gently with the spicy sauce. Cover, reduce the heat to very low and cook for a further 3–4 minutes. You can also use as a layer in lasagne (page 60).

REFRIED BEANS

Another brilliant standby and a must-have accompaniment for many Mexican dishes, such as tacos, quesadillas and tostados. Make a big pot and keep in the fridge. Turn leftovers into a tasty soup by adding stock, chilli and lots of fresh coriander.

SERVES 6–8 V if using butter

450g (1lb) dried or canned black beans, red kidney or pinto beans

110g (4oz) finely chopped onion

1–2 tablespoons good-quality lard or butter

1 teaspoon salt (optional)

a sprig of epazote (optional)

Soak the beans overnight in plenty of water. Alternatively, if you are in a hurry, bring the beans to the boil for 3–4 minutes, then remove from the heat and set aside for an hour or so.

Either way, drain the beans, cover with 1.4 litres (2¼ pints) of fresh water, add the onion and lard or butter. Bring to the boil and simmer gently for 1–2 hours depending on the beans – about 30 minutes before the end of the cooking, add the salt if you want the authentic Mexican flavour and a sprig of epazote if you have it. Top up with boiling water if necessary, the beans should be covered by about 1cm (½in). The beans should be completely soft and the liquid slightly thickish and soupy when they are fully cooked.

THE IMPORTANCE OF STOCK

Stock is a hugely important cook's resource, it's the basis of so many sauces, stews and casseroles. Many people will not have enough bones, carcasses or giblets to make a pot of stock, so keep a 'stock box' in your freezer for carcasses, giblets, vegetable and herb trimmings. When the box is full, make a celebration pot of stock. Cover the pan, otherwise the whole house will smell of stock, which may put you off making it regularly. Don't add potatoes as they soak up flavour and make the stock cloudy. Parsnips and beetroot are too strong and the dye from the latter produces a red stock. Cabbage and other brassicas give an off-taste on long cooking. I also don't add salt because if I want to reduce the stock later to make a sauce, it very soon becomes over-salted.

CHICKEN STOCK

I prefer not to include bay leaf in my chicken stock as I find the flavour can dominate easily and add a sameness to soups made using it later.

MAKES ABOUT 3.5 LITRES (6 PINTS)

2–3 raw or cooked chicken carcasses or a mixture of both
giblets from the chicken (neck, heart, gizzard – save the liver for a different dish), chopped
2 large onions, quartered
1 leek, halved
2 outside celery sticks or 2 lovage leaves
2 large carrots, cut into chunks
a few flat-leaf parsley stalks
a sprig of thyme
6 peppercorns

Put all the ingredients into a large saucepan and cover with about 3.5 litres (6 pints) cold water. Bring to the boil. Skim the fat off the top with a tablespoon. Simmer for 3–4 hours. Strain and remove any remaining fat.

Chicken broth is simply concentrated stock – add a dash of white wine vinegar to release more calcium from the bones.

VARIATIONS

✳ Turkey, pheasant or guinea fowl, goose or duck stock Made in the same way as chicken stock.

✳ Stracciatella Bring 600ml (1 pint) of well-flavoured chicken broth to the boil. Whisk 1 large egg with 1-2 tablespoons of finely grated Parmesan, some salt and a little grated nutmeg in a bowl. Whisk into the boiling broth in a steady stream. The egg will cook into rags on contact with the hot broth. Season to taste.

VEGETABLE STOCK

You can make a vegetable stock from whatever vegetables you have available, but try not to use too much of any one vegetable unless you want that flavour to predominate. As ever the fresher the vegetables, the more flavourful the stock.

MAKES ABOUT 1.8 LITRES (3 PINTS) Ve

1 small white turnip
2 onions, roughly sliced
green parts of 2–3 leeks or spring onions
3 celery sticks, washed and roughly chopped
3 large carrots, scrubbed and roughly chopped
½ fennel bulb, roughly chopped
125g (4½oz) mushroom stalks and peelings
a bouquet garni, including 6 parsley stalks, a sprig of thyme and a scrap of bay leaf
a few black peppercorns
ginger peelings (optional)

Put all the ingredients into a large saucepan. Add 2.5 litres (4½ pints) cold water. Bring to the boil, reduce the heat, cover and leave to simmer for 1–1½ hours. Strain through a sieve.

Vegetable stock keeps for a week in the fridge or may be frozen.

BEEF OR LAMB STOCK

Brown beef stock is used for beef consommé, gravies and sauces. The browning of the bones and vegetables enhances the flavour and colour of the stock. You can use the recipe below to make a more concentrated stock by following the instructions for demi-glace or glace de viande. Lamb stock can be made in a similar way but omit the tomato purée, cloves and garlic.

....

MAKES ABOUT 3.5 LITRES (6 PINTS)

2.7kg (6lb) beef bones or more if you have them, preferably with some nice scraps of meat on them, cut into small pieces

2 large onions, quartered

2 large carrots, quartered

2 celery sticks, cut into chunks

10 peppercorns

2 cloves

4 unpeeled garlic cloves

1 teaspoon concentrated tomato purée

a large bouquet garni, including parsley stalks, bay leaf, sprigs of thyme and a sprig of tarragon

Preheat the oven to 230°C/450°F/ gas mark 8.

Put the beef bones into a roasting tin and roast them for 20–30 minutes until nicely browned. Add the onions, carrots and celery and return to the oven for 10 minutes until the vegetables are coloured at the edges. Transfer the bones and vegetables to a large saucepan with a metal spoon. Add the peppercorns, cloves, garlic, tomato purée and bouquet garni.

Degrease the roasting tin and deglaze with about 300ml (10fl oz) water. Bring to the boil, stir to dissolve the caramelized sediment and then pour over the bones and vegetables in the pan. Add enough additional water to cover the bones, about 4.6 litres (8 pints). Bring slowly to the boil. Skim the stock and simmer gently for 5–6 hours, topping up with water if necessary. Strain the stock, leave it to cool and skim off all the fat before use.

This stock will keep for 2–3 days in the fridge. If you want to keep it for longer, boil it for 10 minutes, and then chill it again. It can also be frozen.

VARIATIONS

✳ **Demi-glace** For a more concentrated stock, return the skimmed stock to a saucepan and boil, uncovered, until reduced by half. It will keep for 3–4 days in the fridge or freeze until needed.

✳ **Glace de viande** Reduce the demi-glace in an uncovered saucepan until it becomes almost syrupy in texture. Pour into a heatproof container and leave to cool. It will set to a firm jelly with a rich, concentrated flavour. Cover and chill. Cut into cubes as needed and use to enrich sauces, stews, casseroles and gravy. It will keep for several weeks, maybe months, in an airtight container in the fridge.

HOW TO TELL WHEN STOCK IS SAFE

It's easy to tell when stock has really gone off, but if it's on the turn, smell it. You might get a slightly suspect whiff. If you're still in doubt, have a taste. Most people's palate will detect a sour taste. If you're still in doubt, put it over the heat. Very often, the smell becomes much more pronounced. But it also becomes slightly foamy on top, and that's a sure sign it's gone off. In the summer, stock should keep for 2–3 days in the fridge; in the winter, 4–5 days. So if you don't intend to use it quite soon, just freeze it. If you think you're going to use it and decide against it, but the stock has been in the fridge for a couple of days, boil it for a few minutes, let it cool again and then refrigerate or freeze it – that should kill off any bacteria.

GOOD TO KNOW ✳ A layer of fat on top seals the stock from the air and means it will keep for longer. Remove the fat before use.

A GREEN SALAD FOR EVERY SEASON

We serve a salad of lettuces, salad leaves, edible flowers and occasional foraged greens with every lunch and dinner at the Ballymaloe Cookery School and it is a much-anticipated part of every meal. The content varies depending on the season but a good green salad will have a contrast of texture, colour and flavour. Seek out salad leaves that have been grown in rich, fertile soil rather than hydroponically, as they will have better flavour and will most likely be more nutritionally complex. Try to grow at least some of your own salad greens if you can, even in a seed tray on your windowsill. Supermarket bagged salad leaves have frequently been washed in a strong chlorine solution, often stronger than in a swimming pool, to kill possible E. coli and salmonella, which isn't so great for your gut health. It is really worth investing in a good salad spinner to dry the leaves otherwise the residual water will dilute the dressing and spoil the salad.

FOR A SPRING SALAD (Ve)

butterhead, iceberg or frisée lettuce; radicchio; chicory; watercress, buckler leaf sorrel; wild and sweet rocket leaves; purslane; wild garlic leaves and flowers; dandelion leaves; pennywort; mibuna; mizuna; salad burnet; golden marjoram; broad bean tips; pea shoots; tiny carrot tops

FOR A SUMMER SALAD (Ve)

butterhead, oakleaf, little gem lettuce, iceberg, lollo rosso or frisée lettuce; mesclun; red orach; mizuna; mibuna; rocket; wild or buckler leaf sorrel; salad burnet; edible chrysanthemum leaves; fresh herb leaves, such as lemon balm, mint, flat-leaf parsley, golden marjoram, annual marjoram, tiny sprigs of dill, tarragon or mint; chive flowers; marigold petals; young nasturtium leaves and flowers; borage or hyssop flowers; courgette or squash blossoms; chickweed; dandelion leaves; yellow kale flowers; watercress flowers; society garlic; green pea shoots or broad bean tips; tiny chard and beetroot leaves

FOR AN AUTUMN OR WINTER SALAD (Ve)

butterhead, oakleaf, lollo or lollo rosso or frisée lettuce; radicchio; chicory; watercress; wild or buckler leaf sorrel; lamb's tongue; wild and sweet rocket leaves; lamb's lettuce; tender leaves of kale; purslane; chickweed; bittercress; pennywort; tips of purple sprouting broccoli, finely shredded; Savoy cabbage, maybe a few shreds of red cabbage and some finely shredded stalks of fresh chard or yellow kale flowers

Wash and carefully dry the lettuce and salad leaves in a salad spinner. Leave whole or, if too large, tear into bite-sized pieces. Put into a deep salad bowl, add the herb sprigs and edible flowers. Toss, cover and chill until needed. Washed organic salad leaves keep perfectly in a plastic bag in the fridge for 4–5 days.

Just before serving, toss the salad in just enough dressing to make the leaves glisten, taste, then add a little more seasoning if necessary.

SALAD DRESSINGS

Dress a green salad just before serving, otherwise it can look tired and unappetizing. The flavour of the dressing totally depends on the quality of the oil and vinegar. I use best-quality, cold-pressed oils and superb wine vinegars to dress the precious organic lettuce and salad leaves we grow at Ballymaloe. The quantity you use is so small it's really worth buying the best quality you can afford – it makes all the difference.

SIMPLE FRENCH DRESSING

MAKES 120ML (4FL OZ) Ve

6 tablespoons cold-pressed extra virgin olive oil
2 tablespoons best-quality white or red wine vinegar
flaky sea salt and freshly ground black pepper

Whisk all the ingredients together just before the salad is to be eaten. Salad dressings are always best when freshly made but this one, which doesn't include raw garlic, shallot or fresh herbs, will keep in a jar in the fridge for 3–4 days. Whisk to emulsify before using.

A tip from Skye Gyngell: Sprinkle 4 tablespoons of grated Parmesan cheese and the zest of ½ lemon over the dressed leaves and serve immediately – utterly delicious!

BALLYMALOE FRENCH DRESSING

MAKES APPROX. 150ML (5FL OZ) V

125ml (4fl oz) extra virgin olive oil
2 tablespoons balsamic or white wine vinegar
1 teaspoon honey
1 garlic clove, crushed
½ teaspoon Dijon mustard
sea salt and freshly ground black pepper

Put all the ingredients into a small bowl or jam jar. Whisk until the dressing has emulsified. Preferably use fresh but it will keep in the fridge for a couple of days. Whisk to emulsify before using.

HERBED VINAIGRETTE DRESSING

MAKES APPROX. 250ML (9FL OZ) V

175ml (6fl oz) extra virgin olive oil
4 tablespoons cider vinegar
1 teaspoon honey
1 garlic clove, crushed
2 tablespoons chopped mixed herbs, such as flat-leaf parsley, chives, mint or thyme
sea salt and freshly ground black pepper

Put all the dressing ingredients into a screw-top jar, adding salt and pepper to taste. Shake well to emulsify before use or whizz together all the ingredients in a food processor or liquidizer for a few seconds. This dressing should be served when freshly made otherwise the herbs will discolour. Or make a day or two ahead without the herbs, then whisk and add the fresh herbs just before serving.

For a variation, use 4 tablespoons of freshly squeezed lemon juice or wine vinegar instead of the cider vinegar. For a Honey & mustard dressing, add 2 teaspoons of Dijon or wholegrain mustard.

POMEGRANATE MOLASSES DRESSING

MAKES APPROX. 210ML (7FL OZ) Ve

2 garlic cloves, crushed
½ teaspoon ground cumin
½ teaspoon granulated sugar
4 tablespoons pomegranate molasses
2 tablespoons freshly squeezed lemon juice
8 tablespoons extra virgin olive oil
sea salt and freshly ground black pepper

Mix the garlic, cumin, sugar, pomegranate molasses and lemon juice together in a bowl. Whisk in the olive oil. Season to taste with salt and pepper. Add a little extra sugar if you think it's a bit too sharp. Preferably use fresh but it will keep in the fridge for a couple of days. Whisk to emulsify before using.

VERJUICE & HONEY VINAIGRETTE

MAKES APPROX. 230ML (8FL OZ) V

50ml (2fl oz) verjuice
1 tablespoon freshly squeezed lemon juice
175ml (6fl oz) extra virgin olive oil
1 teaspoon honey
sea salt and freshly ground black pepper

Whisk all the ingredients together and season to taste.

CAESAR SALAD DRESSING

MAKES APPROX. 400ML (14FL OZ)
50g (2oz) can anchovies
2 organic, free-range egg yolks
1 garlic clove, crushed
2 tablespoons freshly squeezed
    lemon juice
a generous pinch of English mustard
    powder
½ teaspoon salt
½–1 tablespoon Worcestershire
    sauce
½–1 tablespoon Tabasco sauce
175ml (6fl oz) sunflower oil
50ml (2fl oz) extra virgin olive oil

Drain the anchovies and crush lightly
with a fork. Put into a bowl with the
egg yolks, add the garlic, lemon juice,
mustard powder, salt, Worcestershire
and Tabasco sauces. Whisk together
by hand or mix in a food processor.
As you whisk, add the oils slowly at
first, then a little faster as the emulsion
forms. Finally, whisk in 50–110ml
(2–4fl oz) water to give a drizzling
consistency. Season to taste.

TOMATO SALAD

SERVES 4 (V) Remove the cores from 6 very ripe red or
heirloom tomatoes and slice each into 3 or 4 rounds
(around the equator) or into quarters. Arrange in a
single layer on a flat plate. Sprinkle with salt, sugar and
black pepper. Toss immediately in just enough Ballymaloe
French dressing (page 33) to coat the tomatoes and
sprinkle with 1–2 teaspoons of chopped mint or torn basil.
Taste for seasoning. Tomatoes must be dressed as soon as
they are cut to seal in their flavour.

TOMATO SALAD WITH BASIL, OLIVE OIL & HONEY

SERVES 4 (V) Cut 8 very ripe red or heirloom tomatoes into 5mm-(¼
in-)thick slices or quarters or eighths depending on size. Sprinkle
with salt and freshly ground black pepper. Squeeze 2 tablespoons of
lemon juice over the tomatoes. Drizzle with 3 tablespoons of extra
virgin olive oil and 1 tablespoon of honey. Tear over 10–12 basil leaves,
toss gently. Season to taste.

TURKISH TOMATO SALAD

SERVES 6 (Ve) Sprinkle 1 small sliced red onion with 1–2 teaspoons of
sumac and work well into the onion slices with your hands. Leave to
sit while you coarsely chop 6 very ripe tomatoes. Add to the onion
with 2 tablespoons of freshly chopped flat-leaf parsley. Drizzle with
3 tablespoons of extra virgin olive oil and 1–2 tablespoons of lemon
juice, season with flaky sea salt and freshly ground black pepper.
Toss and season to taste – you may need a pinch of sugar.

PICKLED CUCUMBER SALAD

SERVES 4–6 (Ve) Mix 4 tablespoons of granulated sugar, 6 tablespoons
of distilled white vinegar and ½ teaspoon of salt together with
6 tablespoons of water in a saucepan and bring to the boil. Simmer
for 3–5 minutes. When cool, pour the marinade over 1 cucumber,
quartered, deseeded and thinly sliced, 2 thinly sliced shallots and
1 red and 1 green chilli, both deseeded and sliced.

MAYONNAISE

Mayonnaise takes less than 5 minutes to make by hand and it's even quicker in a food processor. It's soooo worth it, just five ingredients as opposed to 18-plus in some well-known brands, one of the main ones is water, so let's hope this recipe will tempt you to have a go at making your own. Mayonnaise is what we call a 'mother sauce' in culinary jargon – the 'mother' of a whole raft of other sauces, so once you can whizz up a mayo, you can make any of the 'daughter' sauces by just adding some extra ingredients. It's good to have all your ingredients at room temperature and drip the oil slowly into the egg yolks at the beginning. The flavour of the mayo totally depends on the quality of the egg yolks, oil and vinegar. The proportion of olive oil to neutral oil is a question of taste.

MAKES 350ML (12FL OZ) Ⓥ

2 organic, free-range egg yolks
¼ teaspoon French mustard
¼ teaspoon salt
1 dessertspoon white wine vinegar
225ml (8fl oz) sunflower or olive oil or a mixture (I use 175ml/6fl oz grapeseed oil and 50ml/2fl oz olive oil)

Put the egg yolks into a bowl with the mustard, salt and the white wine vinegar (keep the whites to make meringues, page 175). Put the oil into a measuring jug. Take a whisk in one hand and the oil in the other and drip the oil on to the egg yolks, drop by drop, whisking at the same time. Within a minute you will notice that the mixture is beginning to thicken. When this happens you can add the oil a little faster, but don't get too cheeky or it will suddenly curdle because the egg yolks can only absorb the oil at a certain pace. Taste and add a little more seasoning and vinegar if necessary.

If the mayonnaise curdles, it will suddenly become quite thin, and if left sitting the oil will start to float to the top of the sauce. If this happens, you can quite easily rescue the situation by putting another egg yolk or 1–2 tablespoons of boiling water into a clean bowl, then whisking in the curdled mayonnaise, ½ teaspoon at a time, until it re-emulsifies.

VARIATIONS

✱ **Aioli** Add 1–4 crushed garlic cloves (depending on size) to the egg yolks as you start to make the mayonnaise. Add 2 teaspoons of chopped flat-leaf parsley at the end and season to taste.

✱ **Saffron or coriander aioli** Substitute ¼ teaspoon of saffron strands soaked in 2 teaspoons of hot water or 1–2 tablespoons of chopped coriander for the parsley in the aioli (above).

✱ **Herb mayonnaise** Add 2–3 tablespoons of chopped dill or coriander to the basic mayo.

✱ **Ginger mayo** Add 1–2 teaspoons of finely grated ginger to the basic mayo.

✱ **Za'atar mayo** Add 1 tablespoon of za'atar to the basic mayo or to taste.

✱ **Wholegrain mustard mayonnaise** Add 1–2 tablespoons wholegrain mustard to the basic mayo.

✱ **Wasabi mayonnaise** Add 1–2 tablespoons of wasabi paste to the eggs instead of mustard and proceed as in the main recipe.

✱ **Tartare sauce** Stir 1 teaspoon of chopped capers, 1 teaspoon of chopped gherkins, 2 teaspoons of chopped chives or chopped spring onions, 2 teaspoons of chopped flat-leaf parsley and the sieved yolks and chopped whites of 2 hard-boiled eggs (page 98) into the basic mayonnaise. Season with salt and pepper.

HOLLANDAISE SAUCE

Like mayonnaise, hollandaise sauce takes less than 5 minutes to make and it transforms any poached fish into a feast – I like to use a coil whisk to make this and other emulsion sauces. Once the sauce is made it must be kept warm: the temperature should not go above 70–80°C (180°F) or the sauce will curdle. A Thermos flask provides a simple solution on a small scale, otherwise put the sauce into a Pyrex or ceramic bowl in a saucepan of hot but not simmering water. Hollandaise sauce cannot be reheated absolutely successfully, so it's best to make the quantity you need. If you do have a little left over, use it to enrich other sauces or mashed potato. I call it hollandaise butter – also delicious melted over pan-grilled fish. If you are making hollandaise sauce for the first time, keep a bowl of cold water close by so you can plunge the bottom of the saucepan into it if becomes too hot.

SERVES 4–6, DEPENDING ON WHAT IT IS TO BE SERVED WITH Ⓥ

2 organic, free-range egg yolks
110g (4oz) butter, diced
approx. 1 teaspoon freshly squeezed lemon juice

Put the egg yolks in a heavy, stainless-steel saucepan over a low heat or in a bowl over hot water. Add 1 dessertspoon of cold water and whisk thoroughly. Add the butter bit by bit, whisking constantly. As soon as one piece melts, add the next piece. The mixture will gradually thicken, but if it shows signs of becoming too thick or slightly scrambling, remove from the heat immediately and add a little cold water if necessary. Do not leave the pan or stop whisking until the sauce is made.

Finally, add the lemon juice to taste. If the sauce is slow to thicken it may be because you are excessively cautious and the heat is too low. Increase the heat slightly and continue to whisk until the sauce thickens to a coating consistency. It is important to remember that if you are making hollandaise sauce in a saucepan directly over the heat, it should be possible to put your hand on the side of the saucepan at any stage. If the saucepan feels too hot for your hand, it is also probably too hot for the sauce.

POP EGGS & WATER INTO A SAUCEPAN

ADD THE BUTTER BIT BY BIT

WATCH THE HEAT

REMOVE FROM THE HEAT & SQUEEZE IN SOME LEMON JUICE

VARIATIONS

✳ Brown butter hollandaise
(Serves 6 –8)
Whisk 2 organic, free-range egg yolks in a bowl. Melt 150g (5oz) butter and continue to cook until it turns brown not black. Pour it in a steady stream on to the egg yolks, whisking continuously until the sauce thickens to a light coating consistency, as in the main recipe. Keep warm in a flask or place in Pyrex bowl (not stainless steel) in a saucepan of hot but not boiling water. Serve with roast or poached fish, asparagus or romanesco.

FLAVOURED BUTTERS

MÂITRE D'HOTEL BUTTER

This is one of the oldest classic flavoured butters, I remember it as a child at the Clarence Hotel in Dublin. It is good served with a piece of pan-grilled fish or steak. Try the various flavoured butters to add an extra pop of flavour and succulence to grills and roast vegetables.

MAKES 110G (4OZ) (V)

110g (4oz) butter
2 tablespoons finely chopped flat-leaf parsley
a few drops of freshly squeezed lemon juice

Cream the butter, then add the parsley and a few drops of lemon juice at a time. Roll into butter pats or form into a roll and wrap in greaseproof paper or foil, screwing each end so that it looks like a Christmas cracker. Refrigerate to harden.

VARIATIONS

* **Fresh herb butter** Substitute a mixture of chopped fresh herbs, such as parsley, chives, thyme, fennel or lemon balm for parsley in the basic recipe. Serve with pan-grilled fish.

* **Mustard & parsley butter** Add 1 tablespoon of Dijon mustard to the basic recipe. Serve with herrings or a juicy steak.

* **Dill or fennel butter** Substitute dill or fennel for parsley in the basic recipe. Serve with fish.

* **Mint or rosemary butter** Substitute 2 tablespoons of finely chopped mint or 1–2 tablespoons of rosemary for the parsley in the basic recipe. Serve with pan-grilled lamb chops.

* **Wild garlic butter** Substitute wild garlic leaves for the parsley. Serve with pan-grilled fish or meat.

* **Watercress butter** Substitute fresh watercress leaves for the parsley. Serve with pan-grilled fish.

* **Garlic butter** Add 3–5 crushed garlic cloves to the basic recipe. Slather over bruschetta or toast. Great with pan-grilled fish, meat or veg.

* **Grainy mustard butter** Cream 110g (4oz) butter, add 1 tablespoon of Dijon mustard and about 2 teaspoons of grainy mustard, put into a bowl and cover or form into a roll and chill until needed. Particularly good with mackerel or herring.

* **Wasabi butter** Add 1–1½ tablespoons of wasabi paste to the basic recipe.

* **Anchovy butter** Mash 6 anchovy fillets into the butter. Serve with pan-grilled fish or fresh radishes.

* **Olive & anchovy butter** Whizz 110g (4oz) butter, 2–3 anchovies, 4 stoned black olives and about 2 teaspoons of chopped flat-leaf parsley together in a food processor or chop ingredients finely and mix with the butter. Cover or form into a roll and refrigerate until needed.

* **Chilli & coriander butter** Cream 110g (4oz) butter, then add 1 finely chopped chilli and 1 tablespoon of chopped coriander or marjoram. Season with freshly ground black pepper and a few drops of lime or lemon juice. Put in a bowl and cover or form into a roll and refrigerate until needed.

* **Cashel or Crozier Blue cheese butter** Mix 110g (4oz) butter, 50g (2oz) blue cheese, 1 teaspoon of black pepper and 1 tablespoon of chopped flat-leaf parsley (optional) in a bowl or whizz in a food processor. Form into a roll in foil or clingfilm. Chill or freeze until needed.

PASTA, RICE, GRAINS

TOASTED NUT & GRAIN GRANOLA

We all need a few tasty breakfast recipes to add pep to our step. Altogether more delicious than virtually any granola you can buy, this recipe is bursting with nutrients – seek out organic grains, fruit and nuts and have fun experimenting with extra fruit, nuts and seeds. Add some coconut flakes, dried banana slices, a teaspoon of ground cinnamon or dried cranberries, cherries or blueberries. If you don't have all the different grains, you can just use 485g (18oz) rolled oats instead. There are two methods here, both crunchy but one deliciously clumpy.

....

SERVES 10 Ⓥ

110ml (4fl oz) light olive or grapeseed oil
175g (6oz) runny honey
235g (8½oz) rolled oats
100g (3½oz) barley flakes
100g (3½oz) wheat flakes
50g (2oz) rye flakes
a pinch of salt
75g (3oz) seedless raisins or sultanas
75g (3oz) almonds, peanuts, hazelnuts or
   cashews, split and toasted
15g (½oz) toasted sunflower and/or
   pumpkin seeds

25g (1oz) chopped dried apricots
45–50g (1¾–2oz) chopped dates (optional)
35g (1¼oz) wheatgerm and/or millet flakes
1 large organic, free-range egg whites (for the
   clumpy version)

TO SERVE

natural yogurt, Jersey milk or milk of your choice
sliced banana or a handful of berries, such as
   raspberries or strawberries

....

Preheat the oven to 180°C/350°F/gas mark 4.

Pour the oil and honey into a saucepan over a low heat and warm just enough to melt the honey. Stir into the oats and flakes, add the salt and mix until well coated. Spread thinly over 1–2 baking sheets and bake for 20–30 minutes. Keep an eye on it and stir the edges into the centre frequently, making sure it doesn't burn. It should be just golden and toasted, not roasted!

Leave to cool completely, then stir in the raisins or sultanas, toasted nuts and seeds, chopped apricots and dates, if using, and add the wheatgerm. Store in a screw-top jar for 2–3 weeks.

For the clumpy granola, break up the egg white with a whisk, add it to the dry ingredients. The fruit needs to

be added at the beginning as it can't really be stirred in at the end because of the clumps. Bake at a lower temperature of 140°C/275°F/gas mark 1 for 4–5 minutes so that the fruit doesn't burn. Leave a space about 23 x 15cm (9 x 6in) in the centre of the tray otherwise the middle won't be fully crisp and golden and you mustn't stir! Leave to cool, then break into clumps. Store in an airtight glass jar for at least 2 weeks.

Serve the granola with sliced banana or some fresh berries in season, or just with a blob of natural yogurt, Jersey milk or milk of your choice.

BALLYMALOE SEASONAL MUESLI

This gem of a recipe is super nutritious and takes just minutes to make. Oats release their carbs slowly so a bowl of muesli will, like porridge, provide lots of energy so you won't feel inclined to grab a doughnut mid-morning. In the summer I make this with ripe seasonal berries – strawberries, raspberries, loganberries and/or tayberries. In autumn, crushed wild blackberries and sweet geranium are delicious added to the grated apples. I particularly love Worcester Pearmain and Cox's Orange Pippin when they ripen in the Ballymaloe orchard, but any sweet dessert apple will be moreish.

SERVES 2 Ⓥ

4 tablespoons organic rolled oats
2 large dessert apples, such as Worcester Pearmain,
  or 4 small apples, such as Cox's Orange Pippin
approx. 1 teaspoon honey
soft brown sugar and a little runny cream, to serve
  (optional)

Measure 3 tablespoons of water into a bowl and sprinkle the oats on top. Let the oats soak up the water overnight or while you grate the apple. A stainless-steel box grater is best for this job, use the largest side and grate the apple coarsely, skin and all. I grate through the core but watch your fingers when you are coming close to the end, pick out the pips and discard.

Stir the honey into the oats and then stir in the grated apple and taste. If it needs a little more honey, add it – this will depend on the sweetness of the apples and how much you heaped up the first spoon. Divide the mixture between two bowls. Have one yourself and give the other to your favourite person that morning! It should taste delicious as is but is even scrummier sprinkled with a little soft brown sugar and a very little runny cream.

GOOD TO KNOW ✱ Depending on the variety, the apple may discolour if it is exposed to the air for a while – it'll still be delicious and nutritious, though.

SEASONAL VARIATIONS

✱ **Apple muesli with chia seeds**
Add 1 tablespoon of chia seeds to the muesli for a high-fibre breakfast.

✱ **Apple & hazelnut muesli**
Add about 1 tablespoon of chopped hazelnuts for extra nutrition and crunch.

✱ **Strawberry muesli** As soon as strawberries come into season, mash about 110g (4oz) ripe berries and use instead of the apple.

✱ **Raspberry, loganberry & tayberry muesli** Swap 110g (4oz) crushed raspberries, loganberries or tayberries for the apple.

✱ **Blackberry & apple muesli**
In autumn, pick some fresh wild blackberries and add to the apple muesli with a few chopped sweet geranium leaves, if you can find them.

ROAST SQUASH & SPELT SALAD

This nourishing salad is inspired by a delicious dish I enjoyed at Roth Bar & Grill in Bruton, Somerset. Serve for a light lunch or as a starter alongside grilled meat or fish.

SERVES 6-10

½ teaspoon chilli flakes
1 teaspoon coriander seeds
1 teaspoon fennel seeds
2 garlic cloves, thinly sliced
1 tablespoon chopped thyme leaves
1 tablespoon chopped rosemary
2 teaspoons chopped marjoram
6 tablespoons extra virgin olive oil, plus extra for drizzling

1 butternut squash (weighing about 1.1kg/2lb 7oz), peeled, deseeded and cut into 2.5cm (1in) cubes
450g (1lb) cherry tomatoes
150g (5oz) pearled spelt
2 tablespoons red wine vinegar
4 tablespoons chopped flat-leaf parsley
40g (1½oz) freshly grated Parmesan cheese
freshly squeezed juice of ½ lemon
1 teaspoon ground coriander
flaky sea salt and freshly ground black pepper

Preheat the oven to 220°C/425°F/gas mark 7.

Grind the chilli flakes, coriander and fennel seeds in a pestle and mortar. Transfer to a bowl and mix with the garlic, thyme, rosemary, half the marjoram and some salt and pepper and the oil. Add the butternut squash and mix well to coat. Spread the squash out in a roasting tin, reserving the remaining flavoured oil.

Halve the cherry tomatoes and toss them in the reserved oil.

Cook the squash for 15–20 minutes until just tender and the edges are golden brown, shaking the tin and turning frequently during cooking. Remove from the oven and leave to cool.

Roast the tomatoes on a separate tray for 3–4 minutes – remove from the oven and leave to cool also.

Put the pearled spelt into a saucepan of cold salted water. Bring to the boil and simmer for 8–10 minutes. Strain, and while still warm, add a generous splash of olive oil, the red wine vinegar, chopped parsley and grated Parmesan.

Mix the squash, tomatoes and spelt together in a clean bowl to gently combine. Add the remaining teaspoon of marjoram, the lemon juice and the ground coriander. Season to taste.

Serve on a large serving platter or on individual plates.

FREEKEH, CUCUMBER, SUMAC & MINT SALAD

Freekeh is a Lebanese wheat which is picked while still underripe and set on fire to remove the husk, which smokes and toasts the grain. It's well worth seeking out and is brilliant for pilaff (page 52), as a side or as a base for a salad such as this one.

SERVES 4-6 Ve

2 tablespoons extra virgin olive oil, plus extra for drizzling
4 garlic cloves, grated
½ teaspoon allspice
a good sprig of thyme
2.5cm (1in) cinnamon stick
150g (5oz) cracked freekeh
2 small or 1 large cucumber

1 medium red onion, halved and thinly sliced
2 tablespoons white wine vinegar
a sprinkling of sugar
30g (1oz) flat-leaf parsley leaves, roughly chopped
20g (¾oz) mint leaves, roughly chopped
zest and juice of 1 medium lemon
approx. 1 teaspoon sumac
flaky sea salt and freshly ground black pepper

Heat the oil in a saucepan over a medium heat. Add the garlic, allspice, thyme sprig and cinnamon. Tip in the freekeh, add 270ml (9½fl oz) water and stir well. Bring to the boil, then simmer gently for 15–20 minutes. Remove from the heat, cover with a lid and leave to sit for 15 minutes.

Meanwhile, prepare the cucumbers. Split lengthways, deseed and cut at an angle into chunks about 2cm (¾in) thick. Put into a bowl with the red onion, vinegar and a sprinkling of salt and sugar. Toss and leave to marinate for 15–20 minutes.

When the freekeh is cold, add to the cucumber with the fresh herbs, lemon zest and juice, a generous drizzle of olive oil and lots of pepper.

Pile on to a serving plate, sprinkle with the sumac and serve as a side or as an accompaniment to grilled lamb, chicken, halloumi or feta.

GOOD TO KNOW ✱ A few halved, super sweet cherry tomatoes would enhance the salad even further.

HOW TO COOK / **PASTA, RICE, GRAINS**

SWEET POTATO, BLACK BEAN & QUINOA CHILLI

Quinoa is a super nutritious grain that originally comes from the Andean region of South America. It is full of protein and has more vitamins and minerals than virtually any other grain, so it's a brilliant option for vegetarians and vegans. Pumpkin or yam may be substituted for the sweet potato in this recipe.

SERVES 4 **V** if using vegetable stock

2 tablespoons extra virgin olive oil
225g (8oz) onion, chopped
2 garlic cloves, crushed
½–1 teaspoon chilli flakes
1 teaspoon ground cumin
1 teaspoon ground coriander
750g (1lb 10oz) sweet potatoes, peeled and
    cut into 2.5cm (1in) dice
450g (1lb) ripe tomatoes, peeled and chopped, or
    400g (14oz) can chopped tomatoes

100g (3½oz) quinoa
500ml (18fl oz) vegetable or chicken stock (page 30)
200g (7oz) black beans, soaked overnight and
    cooked for 1–1½ hours (depending on the age of
    the beans) until just tender or 400g (14oz) can
    black beans, drained and rinsed
a pinch of brown sugar (optional)
4 tablespoons chopped fresh coriander
sea salt and freshly ground black pepper
natural yogurt or labneh (page 113), to serve

Heat the extra virgin olive oil in a sauté pan over a medium heat, add the onion, garlic and chilli flakes and toss together. Reduce the heat, cover and sweat for 5–6 minutes until soft but not coloured. Add the cumin and coriander and season well with salt and pepper.

Add the sweet potatoes, tomatoes, quinoa and stock, bring to the boil and simmer for 10 minutes. Add the black beans and continue to simmer for 20–30 minutes or until the sweet potato and quinoa are tender. Season to taste, you may need to add a little brown sugar if using canned tomatoes.

Serve in a warm bowl scattered with lots of fresh coriander and a dollop of yogurt or labneh.

EVERYDAY DHAL

This truly delicious dhal comes from Ahilya Fort in Maheshwar, one of my favourite places to stay and eat in all of India. They call it Usha Mem Sahib's dhal.

SERVES 6, depending on how it is served

200g (7oz) split red lentils
3 large garlic cloves, thinly sliced on a mandolin
1 ripe tomato, peeled and chopped
110g (4oz) finely chopped onion
2 tablespoons tamarind water (see right)
3 teaspoons ground coriander
1 teaspoon ground cumin
1 teaspoon ground turmeric
1 teaspoon salt
1 tablespoon freshly squeezed lemon juice
2 teaspoons granulated sugar
3 tablespoons fresh coriander, coarsely chopped
natural yogurt and cooked rice, to serve

FOR THE TAMARIND WATER
40g (1½oz) tamarind
150ml (5fl oz) warm water

FOR THE TEMPERING
50g (2oz) clarified butter (page 15) or ghee
3 teaspoons cumin seeds
1 dried red chilli, broken into 5mm (¼in) pieces, or 1 teaspoon chilli flakes
¼ teaspoon ground coriander

To make the tamarind water, soak the tamarind in the warm water for at least 30 minutes, or several hours or overnight if possible, until softened. Push through a sieve and discard the pips. Save any leftover tamarind water in a covered jar in the fridge for another recipe – it keeps for up to 3 months.

Put 900ml (1½ pints) water, the lentils, garlic, tomato, onion, tamarind water, ground coriander, cumin, turmeric and salt into a saucepan over a medium heat. Bring to the boil, then reduce the heat and cook for 18–20 minutes or until the lentils are completely soft. Melt the clarified butter in pan over a medium heat

and add the cumin seeds. When the cumin pops, add the chilli and cook for a minute. Stir in the ground coriander.

Carefully pour the tempering over the lentils as it will sizzle and splash. Cook over a low heat for 3 minutes, add the lemon juice, sugar and chopped coriander and season to taste. Serve with a dollop of natural yogurt on top and some rice alongside.

RAMEN

Ramen is a Japanese noodle soup – the ultimate comfort food; the basic broth needs to be well flavoured but it can be varied in so many ways. The broth can be a mixture of chicken, pork, dashi, miso or vegetable stock. Noodles can be traditional wheat ramen noodles or you can use buckwheat or brown rice noodles for a gluten-free version. The chicken can be substituted for a similar braised brisket or short ribs, pork shoulder, pork belly or bacon, tofu or shrimp. Use whatever vegetables are in season, such as sprouting broccoli, asparagus or shiitake mushrooms. You can also top it with a couple of pieces of nori or a sprinkling of sesame seeds or peanuts. The variations are endless. It's also a fantastic way to use up leftovers at any time of year. Here's a basic starting point.

SERVES 6

1.8 litres (3 pints) homemade chicken stock (page 30)

2 tablespoons dark soy sauce

2 tablespoons mirin

2.5cm (1in) piece of fresh ginger, gently smashed

2 teaspoons toasted sesame oil

300g (10½oz) butternut squash or pumpkin, peeled and cut into 5mm (¼in) pieces

2 red chillies, deseeded and finely sliced

200g (7oz) ramen noodles or noodles of your choice

100g (3½oz) spinach, Swiss chard or kale, roughly chopped

2 tablespoons roughly chopped coriander

freshly squeezed juice of 1 lime

450g (1lb) roast chicken (pages 18–19) or turkey thighs, with or without skin, sliced

3 x 8-minute hard-boiled eggs (page 98)

6 spring onions, thinly sliced on the diagonal

6 lime wedges

sea salt and freshly ground black pepper

Put the chicken stock, soy sauce, mirin and ginger into a saucepan over a medium heat and simmer gently for 5–10 minutes. Discard the ginger. Season with salt and pepper. Add the sesame oil, squash and chillies and simmer for 10 minutes.

Cook the noodles in boiling water according to the packet instructions until just tender. Drain well. Add the spinach to the broth and cook for 1–2 minutes, then add the coriander and lime juice.

Divide the noodles between six bowls and top with the chicken. Ladle the broth over the noodles. Shell the eggs, halve and lay half a 'jammy' egg in each bowl and sprinkle with lots of green spring onions and garnish with a lime wedge. Eat while very hot – broth first and then other ingredients, or any way you want.

GOOD TO KNOW ✳ For extra deliciousness, boil the eggs for 8 minutes, drop into iced water, peel and then submerge in teriyaki sauce. Cover and keep in the fridge overnight.

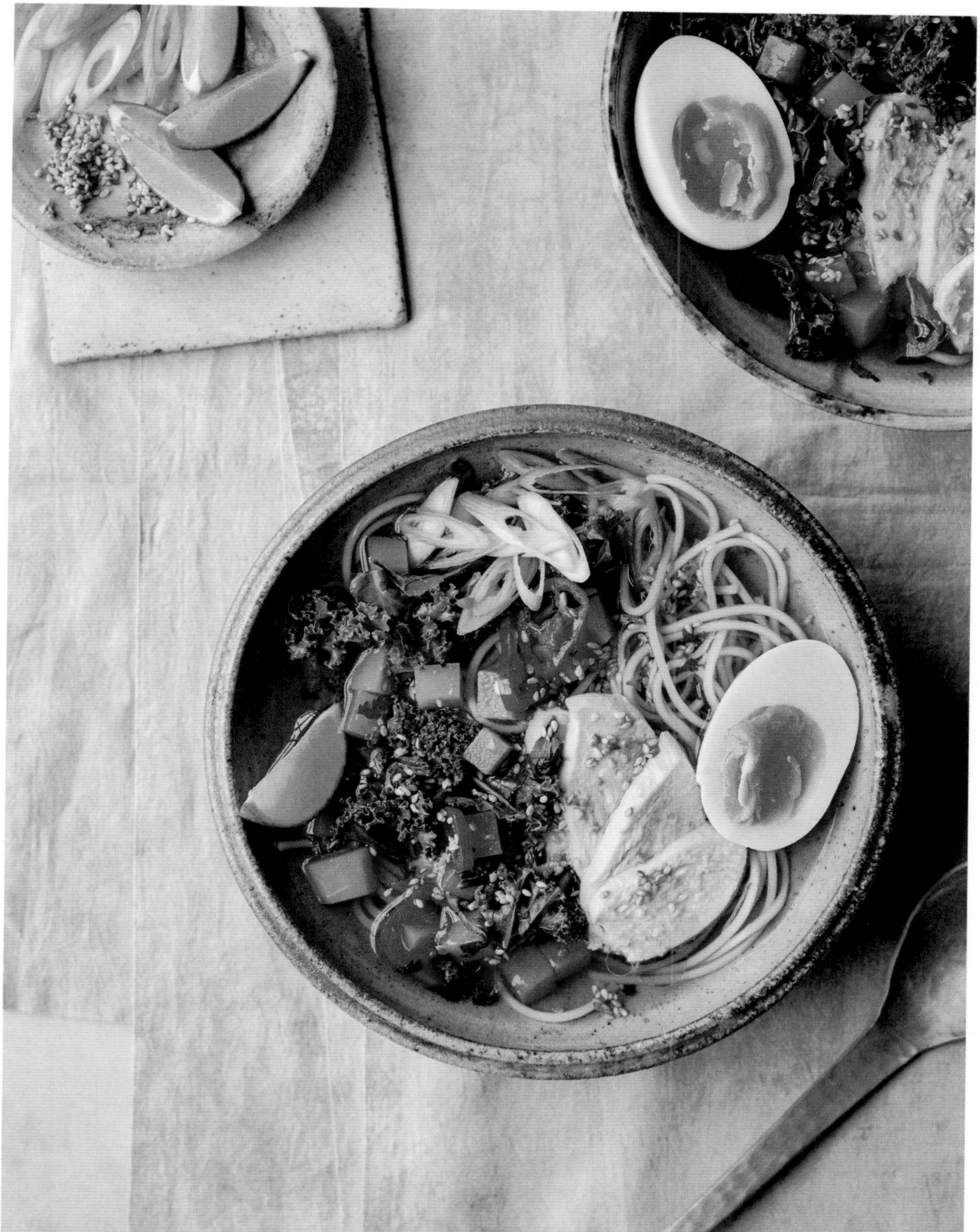

PILAFF RICE

Pilaff rice is even easier to make than a risotto as it looks after itself once the initial cooking is underway, rather than requiring constant stirring. It also earns its place in this book because it's so incredibly versatile. Serve it as a staple or add whatever tasty bits you have to hand – see the suggestions below. Beware, however, of using pilaff as a dustbin, all additions should be carefully seasoned and balanced. You can make it vegetarian or vegan by using vegetable stock and extra virgin olive oil instead of butter. The cooking method also lends itself to a wide variety of grains, including pearl barley, freekeh and spelt (cook according to the packet instructions).

SERVES 8

25g (1oz) butter
2 tablespoons finely chopped onion or shallot
400g (14oz) long-grain rice, preferably best-quality basmati
975ml (1¾ pints) chicken stock (page 30)
2 tablespoons freshly chopped herbs, such as flat-leaf parsley, thyme, chives, a little tarragon (optional)
sea salt and freshly ground black pepper

Melt the butter in a casserole, add the finely chopped onion, cover and sweat for 4–5 minutes. Add the rice and toss for a minute or two, just long enough for the grains to change colour. Season with salt and pepper, add the chicken stock and bring to the boil. Reduce the heat to a minimum, cover and then simmer on the hob or transfer to an oven at 160°C/325°F/gas mark 3 and cook for about 10 minutes. (Basmati rice cooks quite quickly, other types of rice may take up to 15 minutes.) By then the rice should be just cooked and all the liquid absorbed. Just before serving, stir in the fresh herbs, if using.

GOOD THINGS TO ADD TO PILAFF RICE

✱ Gently fold in 2–3 tablespoons of wild garlic a couple of minutes before the end of cooking.

✱ Gently fold in 110–225g (4–8oz) sliced, roast asparagus at the end of cooking. To roast asparagus, drizzle the spears with a little olive oil. Toss gently to coat, season with sea salt, put into a roasting tin and roast at 230°C/450°F/gas mark 8 for 8–10 minutes.

✱ Gently fold in 110–225g (4–8oz) sautéed chestnut or wild mushrooms at the end of cooking.

✱ Fold in 225g (8oz) mussels, cockles, clams, palourdes, shrimps, prawns and 2 tablespoons of dill or fennel close to the end of cooking.

✱ Fold in 110–225g (4–8oz) crisp cubes of bacon, chorizo, merguez sausages or cabonossi close to the end of cooking to heat through.

✱ Fold in 225g (8oz) cooked chicken or game close to the end of cooking to heat through.

✱ Fold in 225g (8oz) roast cubes of squash, pumpkin or courgettes close to the end of cooking to heat through.

✱ Fold in 225g (8oz) cherry tomatoes close to the end of cooking.

CURRIED LENTILS WITH RICE

Another comforting pot, a sort of cross between a dhal and a stew, this is one of my favourite supper dishes. Substitute the natural yogurt with coconut yogurt for a vegan version.

....

SERVES 6-8 Ⓥ

250g (9oz) Puy or brown lentils

4 tablespoons vegetable or olive oil

5 ripe tomatoes (about 450g/1lb), peeled and chopped

1–2 tablespoons jaggery or light soft brown sugar, to taste

400g (14oz) best-quality long-grain rice, such as basmati

a few little knobs of butter (optional)

4 tablespoons natural or coconut yogurt

3 tablespoons chopped coriander, plus sprigs to garnish

flaky sea salt and freshly ground black pepper

FOR THE DRY SPICE MIX

5 green cardamom pods

3 cloves

1½ teaspoons cumin seeds

1 teaspoon ground turmeric

1 bay leaf

2cm (¾in) cinnamon stick

FOR THE WET SPICE MIX

30g (1oz) fresh ginger, peeled and roughly chopped

4 garlic cloves, crushed

1 red or green finger chilli, deseeded and coarsely chopped

....

Put the lentils in a saucepan, cover with 1.5 litres (2½ pints) water and bring to the boil. Cover and simmer for 12–15 minutes or until just tender. Drain and reserve the cooking liquid.

Meanwhile, make the dry spice mix. Remove the seeds from the cardamom pods and crush in a pestle and mortar (discard the pods). Toast with the cloves and cumin seeds in a frying pan over a medium heat for 30 seconds–1 minute. Transfer to a spice grinder (or a pestle and mortar) and whizz or pound to a coarse powder. Pour into a bowl, then add the turmeric, bay leaf and cinnamon stick.

For the wet spice mix, put the ginger, garlic, chilli, onion and 1 teaspoon of salt into a food processor and whizz to a smooth paste. Heat a sauté pan over a medium heat, add the oil and when hot, cook the wet spice mix, stirring, over a medium heat for 8–10 minutes. Add the dry spice mix and cook for 3–4 minutes. Add the chopped tomatoes and season with jaggery or sugar

and salt and pepper. Cook, stirring regularly, for 8–10 minutes or until the oil rises to the top.

To cook the rice, bring 4.5 litres (7¾ pints) water to a fast boil in a large saucepan. Add 1 tablespoon of salt. Sprinkle in the rice and stir. Boil rapidly, uncovered, for 4–5 minutes, then test by biting a few grains between your teeth – it should still have a slightly resistant core. If it overcooks, the grains will stick together later. Strain well through a sieve. Transfer to a warm serving dish, dot with a few knobs of butter, if using, cover with damp baking parchment or a lid and cook at 140°C/275°F/gas mark 1 for at least 15 minutes. Remove the lid and fluff up the rice with a fork to serve.

Add the drained lentils to the spice mixture. Stir and bubble for 3–4 minutes to meld the flavours. Stir in the yogurt and coriander and season to taste. Add some of the lentil cooking liquid (50–150ml/2–5fl oz) to loosen if necessary. Garnish with coriander sprigs and serve with the rice.

SIMPLE SPAGHETTI & MEATBALLS

Meatballs are a universal comfort food, up there with burgers (page 151). This is a really versatile recipe and the meatballs can be used in hot dog buns or sliders. Alternatively, serve them in tomato sauce (page 26) with crusty bread and/or a green salad (page 32).

SERVES 6

FOR THE MEATBALLS

50g (2oz) fresh white breadcrumbs
50ml (2fl oz) whole milk
5 tablespoons extra virgin olive oil
1 onion, finely chopped
1 garlic clove, crushed
900g (2lb) freshly minced beef (20% fat) or
    700g (1½lb) minced beef and 225g (8oz) streaky pork
2–4 tablespoons chopped fresh herbs, such as marjoram, or a mixture of flat-leaf parsley, chives and thyme leaves
1 organic, free-range egg, beaten
sea salt and freshly ground black pepper

FOR THE TOMATO SAUCE

3 tablespoons extra virgin olive oil
225g (8oz) onion, sliced
1 garlic clove, crushed
900g (2lb) ripe, peeled and chopped tomatoes or
    2 x 400g (14oz) cans chopped tomatoes
a good pinch of chilli flakes (optional)
a pinch of sugar
110ml (4fl oz) double cream (optional)

TO SERVE

450g (1lb) spaghetti
150g (5oz) grated mozzarella and Parmesan cheese
a handful of sprigs of flat-leaf parsley or rocket leaves (optional)

Soak the breadcrumbs in the milk. Heat 2 tablespoons of the oil in a heavy, stainless-steel saucepan over a gentle heat and add the onion and garlic. Cover and sweat for 8–10 minutes until soft and slightly golden. Remove from the heat and set aside to cool.

Put the beef and breadcrumbs in a bowl with the cooled onion and garlic, herbs and the beaten egg. Season and mix really well. Fry a tiny bit to check the seasoning, adjust if necessary. Divide into about 24 meatballs on a tray. Cover with baking parchment and refrigerate while you make the sauce.

Heat the oil in a casserole or a stainless-steel saucepan. Add the onion and garlic, toss until coated, cover and sweat over a gentle heat for 5–6 minutes until soft. Add the chopped tomatoes and chilli flakes, if using, mix and season with salt, pepper and a pinch of sugar (canned tomatoes take more sweetening). Add the cream, if using, then cover and simmer for

15 minutes. Remove the lid and cook for a further 15–20 minutes or until the sauce is thick and unctuous.

Heat a frying pan over a medium heat and add the remaining 3 tablespoons of oil. Cook the meatballs for 8–10 minutes, turning from time to time. When they are cooked, transfer to an ovenproof serving dish. Add to the hot tomato sauce, turn gently to cover. Pop into an oven preheated to 180°C/350°F/gas mark 4 and cook for 8–10 minutes.

Meanwhile, cook the spaghetti in a pan of boiling salted water according to the packet instructions. Drain and turn into a hot serving dish.

Spoon the meatballs and tomato sauce over the spaghetti and sprinkle with mozzarella and Parmesan. Serve garnished with flat-leaf parsley or rocket leaves. Alternatively, place under a preheated grill to melt the cheese and sprinkle with the parsley or rocket leaves.

EVERYONE'S FAVOURITE MAC & CHEESE

Mac and cheese is a bit like apple crumble, simple fare but everyone loves it, plus you can add lots of tasty bits to change it up. Macaroni cheese was and still is one of my children's favourite supper dishes. I often add some cubes of cooked bacon or ham to the sauce.

SERVES 6 Ⓥ if not using Parmesan

225g (8oz) macaroni or ditalini
50g (2oz) butter
150g (5oz) onion, finely chopped
50g (2oz) plain flour
850ml (1½ pints) boiling whole milk
¼ teaspoon Dijon or English mustard
1 tablespoon chopped flat-leaf parsley (optional)
225g (8oz) freshly grated mature Cheddar cheese or a mix of Cheddar, Gruyère and Parmesan
25g (1oz) freshly grated Cheddar or Parmesan cheese, for sprinkling on top (optional)
sea salt and freshly ground black pepper

Bring 3.4 litres (6 pints) water to the boil in a large saucepan and add 2 teaspoons of salt. Sprinkle in the macaroni and stir to make sure it doesn't stick together. Cook according to the packet instructions until just soft. Drain well.

Meanwhile, melt the butter over a gentle heat, add the chopped onion, stir to coat, cover and sweat over a gentle heat for 6–8 minutes. Add the flour and cook over a medium heat, stirring occasionally, for 1–2 minutes. Remove from the heat. Whisk the milk in gradually, season well with salt and pepper, then return to the boil, stirring constantly. Add the mustard, parsley, if using, and cheese. Add the well-drained macaroni and return to the boil. Season to taste and serve immediately.

Alternatively, turn into a 1.2-litre (2-pint) pie dish and sprinkle the extra grated cheese over the top. Bake at 180°C/350°F/gas mark 4 for 15–20 minutes.

GOOD THINGS WITH MAC & CHEESE

✳ **Mac & cheese fritters** Heat olive oil in a deep-fat fryer at 180°C (350°F) or a deep saucepan with 5–7.5cm (2–3in) depth of oil. Roll the leftover mac and cheese into ping-pong-sized balls. Roll in seasoned flour, beaten eggs and fresh white or panko crumbs to coat. Fry for 4–5 minutes until crisp on the outside and melting in the interior. Remove with a slotted spoon, drain on kitchen paper and toss in freshly grated Parmesan. Serve with spicy mayo made by mixing 110ml (4fl oz) homemade mayonnaise (page 35) with 3 teaspoons of sriracha, 2 teaspoons of sambal oelek or harissa and lemon juice to taste. Alternatively, allow the baked mac and cheese to get cold in the gratin dish. Cut into fingers or squares, dip in seasoned flour, egg and breadcrumbs and shallow-fry in olive oil for 3–4 minutes until crisp and golden on both sides. Serve with a dipping sauce or with the spicy mayo.

✳ **Smoked salmon or smoked mackerel** Add 225g (8oz) smoked salmon or smoked mackerel dice to the mac and cheese before serving.

✳ **Mushrooms & courgettes** Add 225g (8oz) sliced sautéed mushrooms and 225g (8oz) sliced courgettes cooked in olive oil with a little garlic and marjoram or basil to the cooked mac and cheese. Toss gently, turn into a hot serving dish and scatter with grated cheese and serve or reheat later.

✳ **Chorizo** Add 225g (8oz) diced chorizo and lots of chopped flat-leaf parsley to the mac and cheese before baking.

PASTA E CECI

Ditalini is the Italian name for very short macaroni, sometimes called tubetti – keep some in your pantry and use for pasta e fagioli (pasta and beans), mac and cheese (opposite) or simply toss it in tomato (page 26) or your favourite pasta sauce.

SERVES 4–6

3 tablespoons extra virgin olive oil, plus extra
   for drizzling
175g (6oz) onions, finely chopped
3 garlic cloves, finely chopped
2 teaspoons chopped rosemary
½ teaspoon chilli flakes
400g (14oz) can chopped tomatoes
400g (14oz) can chickpeas, drained
110g (4oz) ditalini pasta
4 handfuls of radicchio, cavolo nero or escarole,
   roughly chopped
50g (2oz) freshly grated Pecorino cheese
flaky sea salt and freshly ground black pepper

Heat the oil in a sauté pan over a medium heat. Add the chopped onions, toss and cook for 4–5 minutes until soft and mellow but not coloured. Add the garlic, rosemary, chilli flakes and cook for a further minute or two. Season with salt and pepper. Add the chopped tomatoes and chickpeas, bring to the boil, add 675ml (1¼ pints) water and the pasta and bring back to the boil and cook for about 10 minutes until the pasta is al dente. Most of the water will be absorbed by the pasta. Season to taste with salt and pepper.

Add the roughly chopped greens and cook until wilted, then season to taste.

Ladle into a bowl, drizzle with your best extra virgin olive oil and sprinkle with grated Pecorino cheese.

CHEAT'S METHOD OF COOKING DRIED PASTA

We developed this method of cooking pasta when we taught a 'survival' course for students in small apartments with limited cooking facilities (maybe just one gas ring). Italians are usually shocked, but it works brilliantly. Use a similar method for cooking rice.

Choose a large, deep saucepan; two handles are an advantage for ease of lifting. To cook 500g (18oz) pasta, use 2 tablespoons of sea salt to 4.5 litres (7½ pints) of water. Bring the water to the boil before adding the salt and the pasta. Tip the pasta in all at once and stir well to ensure the strands are separate, then cover the pan just long enough to bring the water back to the boil. Cook for 2 minutes for noodles, spaghetti and tagliatelle, 4 minutes for penne, small shells, etc. Keep the pan covered. Then turn off the heat and allow the pasta to continue to cook for the time indicated on the packet. (Meanwhile, make a sauce.) Test, drain and proceed as usual. This method is good and does not overcook the pasta as easily as when it is cooked the conventional way.

VEGETABLE LASAGNE

Lasagne is basically just a formula and once you've learned that you can start to play around and have fun making it with a variety of different vegetarian or meat fillings. Try Tomato fondue (page 27) instead of the Piperonata and ricotta in place of the Mushroom à la crème and cook as below. Or use Spiced Aubergines (page 29) instead of the Piperonata.

....

SERVES 12 Ⓥ if not using Parmesan

375g (13oz) plain or spinach lasagne sheets
1 x Piperonata (page 26)
2 x Mushroom à la crème (page 28)
225g (8oz) freshly grated Parmesan or mature
   Cheddar cheese or a mixture of both

2 small sprigs of thyme
2 small sprigs of flat-leaf parsley
270g (10oz) roux made with 135g (4½oz)
   butter and 135g (4½oz) plain flour
sea salt and freshly ground black pepper

FOR THE BÉCHAMEL SAUCE

1.8 litres (3 pints) cold whole milk
1 carrot, sliced
1 onion, sliced
6 peppercorns

FOR THE BUTTERED SPINACH

900g (2lb) spinach, Swiss chard or kale,
   stalks removed, washed and drained
50–110g (2–4oz) butter, according to taste
a little freshly grated nutmeg

....

Preheat the oven to 180°C/350°F/gas mark 4.

Blanch the lasagne sheets as directed on the packet, if necessary.

To make the béchamel sauce, put the milk into a saucepan with the carrot, onion, peppercorns, thyme and parsley. Bring to the boil, then simmer for 4–5 minutes. Remove from the heat and leave to infuse for 10 minutes. Melt the butter over a low-medium heat to make a roux. Add the flour, stir and cook over a medium heat until it becomes the consistency of wet sand. Stir and cook for about 2 minutes. Strain out the vegetables, bring the milk back to the boil and whisk in the roux to thicken. Season with salt and pepper to taste.

To make the buttered spinach, melt 1 tablespoon of the butter in a wide frying pan, toss in as much spinach as will fit easily and season with salt and pepper. As soon

as the spinach wilts and becomes tender, strain off all the liquid, increase the heat and add the remaining butter and freshly grated nutmeg.

Spread a little béchamel sauce on the base of a 30 x 20 x 6cm (12 x 8 x 2½in) lasagne dish or two 21 x 13.5 x 4.5cm (8½ x 5½ x 1¾in) dishes, cover with lasagne, then Piperonata. Top with another layer of lasagne. Spread with half the remaining béchamel sauce, sprinkle with half the grated cheese and add the buttered spinach. Cover with another layer of pasta, then the mushroom à la crème, then top with a layer of lasagne. Carefully spread the remaining béchamel sauce over the lot and finally sprinkle liberally with the remaining cheese. (Make sure all the pasta is under the sauce.) Clean the edges of the dish with a cloth. Bake for 30 minutes or until golden and bubbly on top. If possible, leave to stand for 10–15 minutes before cutting to allow the layers to compact. Serve with a good green salad (page 32).

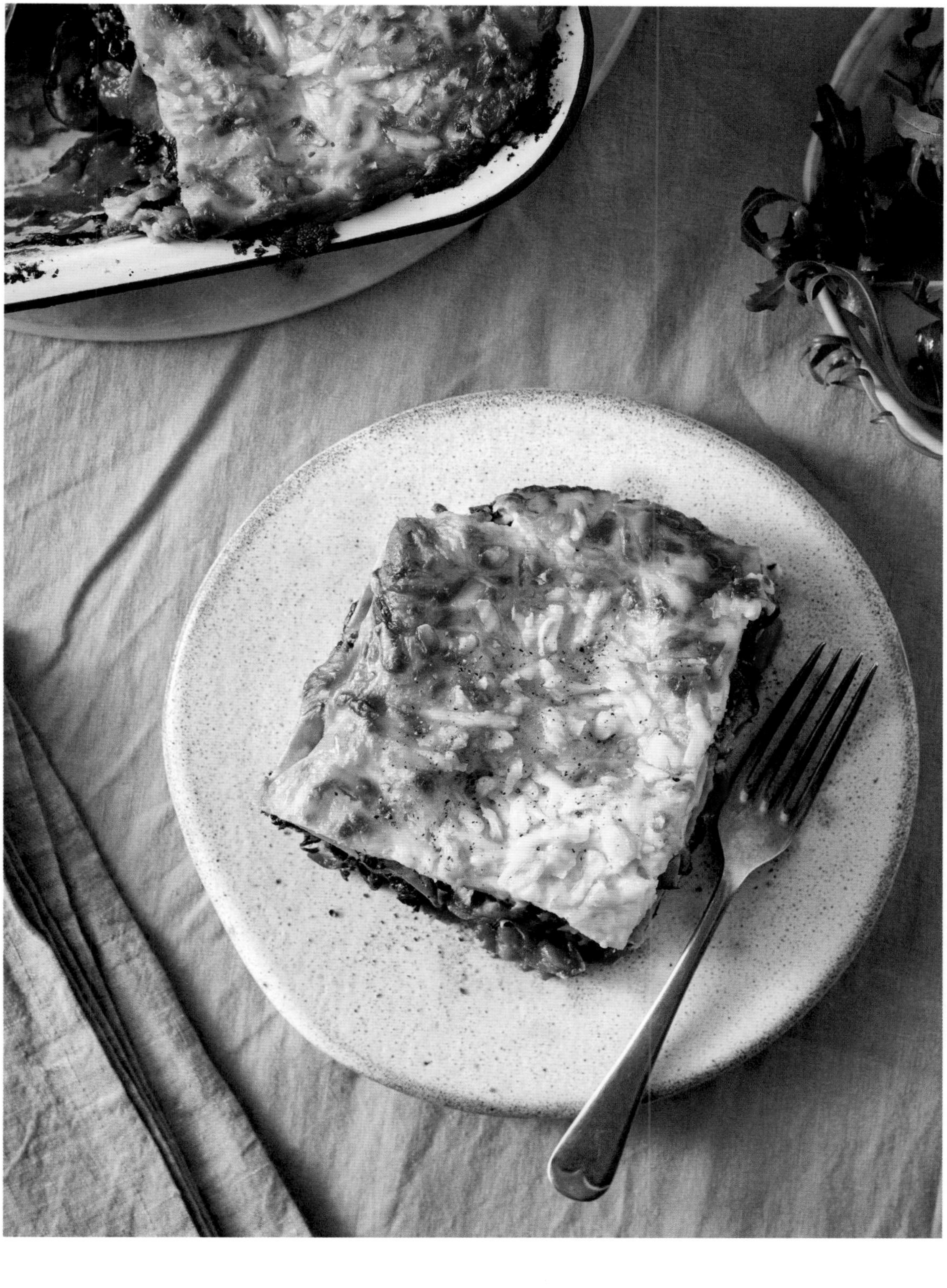

VEGETABLES

BEETROOT 'HUMMUS'

I'm using poetic licence here when I call
this beetroot purée 'hummus' but it's
a riff on a recipe that Yotam Ottolenghi
shared with us on one of his visits to the
Ballymaloe Cookery School. This is best
made in the summer when the beets
are young, sweet and tender.

SERVES 4–6 **V**

450g (1lb) medium beetroot, washed
2 garlic cloves, crushed
½–1 small red chilli, deseeded and finely chopped
125g (4½oz) natural yogurt
3 teaspoons date syrup
1½ tablespoons extra virgin olive oil, plus
   extra for drizzling
½–1 tablespoon za'atar (depending on freshness)
1–2 teaspoons honey (optional)
salt

TO GARNISH

1 spring onion, green and white parts, thinly sliced
10g (½oz) pistachios, coarsely chopped
30g (1oz) soft goat's cheese, crumbled
marigold petals (optional)

Cook the beetroot in boiling, well-salted water for
30 minutes–1 hour until the skins rub off and a skewer
can pierce the beetroot easily. Once it is cool enough
to handle, rub off the skin. Cut into chunks and
whizz to a smooth purée in a food processor with the
garlic, chilli and yogurt. Transfer to a bowl, stir in the
date syrup, oil, za'atar and about 1 teaspoon of salt.
Taste and add more salt and the honey if necessary.
Transfer to a bowl or serving plate. Scatter over the
spring onions, pistachios and top with little blobs of
goat's cheese. Drizzle with a little oil. Serve at room
temperature and sprinkle with marigold petals, if using.
Store for 6–7 days in the fridge.

HUMMUS BI TAHINA

Hummus is so delicious and easy to
make, you'll never be tempted to buy
it again. Serve with pitta bread, kebabs
or as part of a mezze spread.

MAKES 600G (1¼LB)/SERVES 4–8 depending on how it is served

175g (6oz) dried chickpeas, soaked overnight in
   600ml (1 pint) water or 2 x 400g (14oz) cans
1 teaspoon bicarbonate of soda
freshly squeezed juice of 2–3 lemons, to taste
2–3 large garlic cloves, finely crushed
150ml (5fl oz) tahini
1 teaspoon ground cumin (optional)
2 tablespoons coarsely chopped flat-leaf
   parsley (optional)
approx. 60ml (2½fl oz) iced water
salt
pitta bread or any crusty white bread, to serve

Drain the chickpeas and put in a medium saucepan
over a high heat. Sprinkle with the bicarbonate of
soda, stir and cook for about 3 minutes. Add 1.5 litres
(2½ pints) water and bring to the boil. Cook for
20–40 minutes, skimming off any foam. The chickpeas
are cooked when they are really soft but not mushy.

Drain the chickpeas, discarding any loose skins. Save
the cooking liquid. (If using canned chickpeas, drain
– saving the liquid – and continue, adding back in the
liquid plus some iced water if needed.) Whizz in a food
processor with the lemon juice and a little reserved
cooking water if necessary. Add the garlic, tahini,
cumin (if using) and salt to taste. Blend to a soft, silky
paste. Taste and continue to add lemon juice and salt
until you are happy. Add the iced water and whizz until
completely smooth. Sprinkle a couple of chickpeas, a
drizzle of paprika oil (page 100) and a little chopped
parsley over the top, as you wish. Store in a covered
container in the fridge for up to 3 days.

OAXACAN BLACK BEAN SALAD

I love this perky Mexican salad and make it throughout the year with either fresh or canned sweetcorn.

SERVES 6–8 Ve

- 2 x 400g (14oz) cans black beans, rinsed and drained, or 450g (1lb) black beans, soaked overnight and cooked for 30 minutes
- 175–225g (6–8oz) cooked fresh sweetcorn or corn niblets
- 2 red peppers, deseeded and diced
- 2 garlic cloves, crushed or grated
- 2 tablespoons shallots, finely chopped
- 2 teaspoons salt
- ¼ teaspoon cayenne pepper
- 125g (4½oz) chopped fresh coriander, plus extra to garnish
- 2 ripe but firm avocados, diced (preferably Hass)
- corn tortilla chips, to serve

FOR THE DRESSING

- 9 tablespoons extra virgin olive oil
- 1 teaspoon lime zest
- 6 tablespoons freshly squeezed lime juice
- 2 tablespoons granulated sugar

Put the black beans, sweetcorn, red peppers, garlic and shallots into a bowl. Sprinkle over the the salt, cayenne and chopped coriander. Toss gently to combine.

Mix the extra virgin olive oil with the lime zest and juice. Add the sugar and whisk to emulsify. Pour over the salad and toss. Season to taste and add a little more sugar if necessary to balance the lime.

Just before serving, add the avocados and mix gently. Garnish with coriander and serve at room temperature with lots of tortilla chips on the side.

CARROT & SPRING ONION FRITTERS

These vegetarian spiced fritters can be vegan if you omit the egg. Change the vegetables with the seasons: try cabbage, parsnips, celeriac or sprouts.

MAKES 16/ SERVES 4

- 80g (3¼oz) chickpea (gram) flour
- 4 tablespoons self-raising flour
- 2 teaspoons ground coriander
- 2 teaspoons ground cumin
- ½ teaspoon paprika plus ½ teaspoon smoked paprika
- 1 organic, free-range egg (optional)
- 150g (5oz) carrots, grated
- 30g (1oz) spring onions, thinly sliced
- extra virgin olive oil, for frying
- flaky sea salt and pepper
- Coriander aioli (page 35), to serve

Mix together the flours, spices and a generous pinch of salt in a bowl. Whisk the egg with 110ml (4fl oz) water. (For a vegan version, omit the egg and increase the water to 150ml/5fl oz). Add to the dry ingredients and mix together – the batter should be the texture of double cream. If it's too thick, add a little more water. Cover loosely with a tea towel and leave to stand for 30 minutes.

Add the carrots and spring onions to the batter, stir and season until the vegetables are well coated.

Heat a little olive oil in a non-stick frying pan over a medium heat. Drop a tablespoon of the mixture into the pan. Fry for 2–3 minutes on each side until golden brown and crispy on the outside and cooked in the centre. Season to taste. Fry three or four at a time, depending on the pan size. Serve 3–4 fritters per person on hot plates with Coriander aioli alongside.

WHITE BEAN STEW
WITH TOMATOES & ROSEMARY

This bean stew freezes brilliantly in all its incarnations – see Variations below.
Serve as a vegetarian main or as a side dish to roast lamb or pork, or roast vegetables.

SERVES 4–6 Ve

225g (8oz) dried haricot beans or cannellini beans
bouquet garni made from a bay leaf, parsley stalks,
   thyme, celery stick (optional)
1 onion, halved
1 carrot, halved
175g (6oz) chopped onion

3 tablespoons olive oil
4 large cloves garlic, crushed
400g (14oz) can chopped tomatoes
a large sprig of rosemary, chopped
sea salt and freshly ground black pepper
sugar

Soak the beans overnight in plenty of cold water.
Next day, strain the beans and cover with fresh cold
water, add the bouquet garni, onion and carrot,
cover and simmer for 30 minutes–1 hour until the
beans are soft but not mushy. Just before the end
of cooking, add salt to taste. Remove the bouquet
garni and vegetables and discard. Save the cooking
liquid for later.

Meanwhile, sweat the chopped onion gently in the
oil in a wide saucepan for 7–8 minutes until soft but
not coloured, add the garlic and cook for a further
minute or two. Then add the chopped tomatoes,
cooked white beans and rosemary. Simmer for
10–15 minutes – add some of the bean liquid if
necessary and season well with salt, freshly ground
black pepper and sugar. The mixture should be
loose and juicy but not swimming in liquid.

VARIATIONS

* **Haricot beans with tomatoes,
rosemary & cauliflower** Blanch and refresh
450g (1lb) cauliflower or broccoli florets,
add to the main recipe 5 minutes before the
end of cooking.

* **Haricot beans with tomatoes,
rosemary & chilli** Add 1 chopped red or
green chilli to the chopped onions and
proceed as in the main recipe.

* **Haricot beans with tomatoes
& rosemary with chorizo** Add 1 chorizo,
sliced, to the tomato base with the beans
and rosemary.

* **Gratin of haricot beans with tomatoes
& rosemary** Put the mixture into a shallow
ovenproof dish. Scatter a mixture of
buttered crumbs (page 75) and approx.
50g (2oz) grated Cheddar cheese (or a
mixture of Cheddar and Parmesan or other
well-flavoured cheeses) over the top and
put into a hot oven or flash under a grill
until crisp and golden on top.

FALAFEL WITH TAHINI SAUCE

We're all addicted to falafel and there are many variations on this basic recipe, so get started and then play around: add dill, chilli powder, turmeric, maybe a little smoked paprika or roll the falafel in sesame seeds. Delicious served with a dollop of creamy hummus (page 64) or tzatziki.

MAKES APPROX. 20

½ onion (approx. 60g/2¼oz)
1 garlic clove, peeled
1 green chilli
a small handful of flat-leaf parsley leaves
a small handful of coriander leaves
125g (4½oz) dried chickpeas, soaked in
  plenty of cold water overnight and drained
½ teaspoon ground cumin
⅓ teaspoon ground cardamom
½ teaspoon salt
scant ¼ teaspoon freshly ground black pepper
2 tablespoons chickpea (gram) or plain flour
1 teaspoon baking powder

FOR THE TAHINI SAUCE (Makes approx. 250g/9oz)

125g (4½oz) tahini
1 garlic clove, crushed
a generous pinch of salt
juice of 1 large lemon

Put the onion, garlic, chilli and herbs into a food processor, pulse to roughly chop, then add the chickpeas and whizz to a thick, coarse purée. You'll probably need to scrape the sides down, then pulse again to make sure everything is a similar texture but do not over-blitz. To check, scoop up a small amount and squeeze it in your hand – it should hold its shape. If not, whizz for another few seconds. Transfer to a large bowl, add the spices, salt, pepper, chickpea flour and baking powder and mix well until thoroughly combined.

To make the tahini sauce, whizz the tahini, garlic, salt and lemon juice in a food processor. Add 60ml (2½fl oz) water, it will block up but don't worry – just continue to add up to another 60ml (2½fl oz) water, it will loosen to a creamy texture. If the mixture becomes too runny, add a little extra tahini. Add a little more salt and/or lemon juice to taste. The sauce will keep in an airtight container in the fridge for 2–3 days but is best enjoyed fresh.

Preheat a deep-fat fryer to 170°C (325°F). Cook a little blob of falafel to test for seasoning and tweak if necessary.

Now you have a choice – falafel can be shaped in a few different ways. Wet your hands with cold water, shape the mixture into walnut-sized balls, torpedo shapes or into flat patties for falafel burgers. Slide them carefully into the hot oil – not too many at a time – and fry for 2–3 minutes until the exteriors are brown and crunchy. Drain on kitchen paper and serve immediately. Enjoy with the tahini sauce and sliced tomatoes, spring onions, lettuce and/or flatbread, as you wish.

VEGGIE TOAD IN THE HOLE

A super versatile one-dish meal.

SERVES 8 **V**

4 medium onions, quartered

3 large carrots (500g/18oz) peeled, halved lengthways and cut into 1cm (½in) pieces

6 small-medium beetroot (500g/18oz), cut into 1cm (½in) wedges

4 medium potatoes (500g/18oz), washed and cut into 1cm (½in) wedges

3 garlic cloves, grated

2 teaspoons ground cumin

2 teaspoons ground coriander

1 level teaspoon chilli flakes

1 level teaspoon flaky sea salt

freshly ground black pepper

6 tablespoons extra virgin olive oil

4 organic, free-range eggs, lightly beaten

300ml (10fl oz) whole milk

30g (1oz) butter, melted

225g (8oz) plain flour

4 tablespoons freshly chopped herbs, such as flat-leaf parsley, thyme, chives and marjoram or tarragon or 4 tablespoons freshly chopped dill, plus parsley, to garnish

Preheat the oven to 230°C/450°F/gas mark 8.

Put the prepared vegetables into a large bowl. Mix the garlic, spices and the seasoning with the oil. Pour over the vegetables and toss well so each piece is coated with the spicy oil. Turn into a 32.5 x 22.5 x 5cm (8 x 9 x 2in) gratin dish and roast for 30–35 minutes or until almost tender and the edges are slightly caramelized.

Meanwhile, whizz the eggs, milk and butter, flour and herbs in a blender or food processor. Alternatively, sift the flour into a bowl, make a well in the centre and drop in the eggs. Using a small whisk or wooden spoon, stir continuously, gradually drawing in flour from the sides, adding the milk in a steady stream at the same time. When all the flour has been incorporated, whisk in the cool melted butter and freshly chopped herbs. Season well with salt and pepper.

When the roast vegetables are three-quarters cooked, pour the batter into the hot gratin dish, pop back into the oven and bake for a further 15–20 minutes.

VARIATIONS

✶ Roast vegetable & sausage toad in the hole Allow the batter to stand while you cook pork, frankfurters or Toulouse or merguez sausages in a very little oil in a frying pan until pale golden on all sides. Slice the cooked sausages and mix through the vegetables and pour into a small roasting tin. Heat on the hob for a few seconds and when it begins to sizzle, pour in the batter. Bake in the oven at 230°C/450°F/gas mark 8 for 20–25 minutes or until well risen and crisp. Sprinkle with chopped parsley and serve.

✶ Individual toad in the hole Heat a 12-hole muffin tray in the hot oven. Grease with olive oil, spoon-fill each hole three-quarters full with roast vegetables (and sausage slices – optional). Cover with the batter. Top with a little grated Cheddar cheese and cook in the oven at 230°C/450°F/gas mark 8 for 15–20 minutes or until puffed and golden.

ROAST SUMMER VEGETABLE TRAYBAKE

The crunchy roast chickpeas and herby dressing add extra magic to this traybake of simple summer veg. The chickpeas are seriously addictive – I've used freshly ground cumin and coriander here but garam masala, smoked paprika, chilli powder, chopped rosemary or thyme leaves are also delicious. The chickpeas will get crispier as they cool. Enjoy as a nibble or sprinkle over salads or roast vegetables.

SERVES 4–6 **V** if using halloumi

extra virgin olive oil

4 Hungarian wax chillies or 8 Turkish peppers

2 red onions, sliced

8 broad beans in their pods

12 peas in their pods

6 young carrots, split lengthways

8 French breakfast radishes

Aleppo pepper or Piment d'Espelette

150g (5oz) halloumi or feta cheese, cut into 2.5cm-(1in-)thick fingers

zest and juice of 1 lemon

1 tablespoon thyme leaves

sea salt and freshly ground black pepper

FOR THE SPICY ROAST CHICKPEAS

400g (14oz) can chickpeas

1–2 teaspoons each of cumin and coriander seeds, toasted and ground (optional)

FOR THE DRESSING

2 tablespoons chopped mint

2 tablespoons chopped dill

2 tablespoons chopped flat-leaf parsley

4 tablespoons extra virgin olive oil

1 tablespoon white wine vinegar

1 teaspoon honey

Preheat the oven to 220°C/425°F/gas mark 7.

Drain the chickpeas, rinse under cold water and drain again. Lay on kitchen paper, shake and pat gently until dry. Spread the chickpeas out in a single layer on a small baking tray, drizzle with extra virgin olive oil. Sprinkle generously with sea salt and the cumin and coriander seeds (if using). Shake to coat. Roast for 25–30 minutes or until crisp and golden. Cool, taste, add more salt and spices if necessary. Store in an airtight jar. Increase the oven temperature to 230°C/450°F/gas mark 8.

Put all the vegetables in a bowl, drizzle with extra virgin olive oil and season with salt, pepper and lots of chilli pepper flakes. Spread out in a roasting tin and cook for 20 minutes until the edges of the vegetables are beginning to caramelize and char.

Heat a little oil in a pan over a medium heat and cook the cheese until it is golden on each side. Alternatively, cook in a block on the edge of the vegetable tray for 15–20 minutes, turning halfway through cooking.

Meanwhile, whisk the freshly chopped herbs, oil, vinegar and honey together for the dressing.

When the vegetables are almost cooked but still slightly al dente, sprinkle with the lemon zest and thyme leaves. Squeeze half a lemon over the top, toss and return to the oven for a couple of minutes.

Pile on to plates and top with the cheese. Sprinkle liberally with the herb dressing and crunchy chickpeas. Serve with lots of flatbread to mop up the juices.

ROAST WINTER VEGETABLES

This gratin tastes different every time I make it. A versatile technique that can be vegetarian or vegan with added tofu, or you can include chunks of bacon or spicy sausage. Remember you don't need all these vegetables, just three or four would be brilliant – gutsy winter herbs really add oomph! Substitute 1 teaspoon each of cumin, coriander and maybe some smoked paprika for the herbs if desired.

....

SERVES 8 Ve

2kg (4½lb) winter vegetables of your choice from:
    carrots, peeled and cut into 4cm (1½in) pieces
    parsnips, peeled and cut into 4cm (1½in) pieces
    pumpkin or butternut squash, peeled and
        cut into 4cm (1½in) pieces
    Jerusalem artichokes, peeled and
        cut into 4cm (1½in) pieces
    red or white onion, peeled and cut into
        wedges of quarters or sixths, depending on size
    leeks, cut into 2.5cm (1in) rounds
    beetroot, peeled and cut into 4cm (1½in) pieces
    celeriac, peeled and cut into 4cm (1½in) pieces

8 garlic cloves, unpeeled
extra virgin olive oil
1–2 tablespoons rosemary and/or
    thyme, freshly chopped
flaky sea salt and freshly ground black pepper

....

Preheat the oven to 230°C/450°F/gas mark 8.

Toss the prepared vegetables into the gratin dish, drizzle with extra virgin olive oil and season with salt and pepper. Sprinkle with freshly chopped herbs. Toss well so each chunk is lightly coated. Roast for 30–40 minutes, tossing occasionally, or until the vegetables are fully cooked and starting to caramelize at the edges. Serve immediately.

Tuck in as soon as the roast vegetables come out of the oven, if they sit around in or out of the oven, they'll quickly go soggy and you may wonder why you bothered.

LEEK, SPROUT & MACARONI BAKE

This gratin can be cooked ahead, refrigerated for several days or frozen, so it's a good standby option. Try adding some little morsels of bacon, chorizo, merguez or Toulouse sausage, all add extra magic and nutrients. This gratin is also delicious alongside cold meats, particularly ham or bacon.

SERVES 8–10

110g (4oz) macaroni
450g (1lb) Brussels sprouts, weighed after trimming, cut into quarters
25g (1oz) butter
450g (1lb) leeks (white and green parts sliced in 7mm/¼in slices at an angle)
sea salt and freshly ground black pepper
green salad (page 32), to serve

FOR THE MORNAY SAUCE

50g (2oz) butter
50g (2oz) plain flour
900ml (1½ pints) boiling whole milk
1 teaspoon Dijon mustard
1 tablespoon chopped flat-leaf parsley (optional)
150g (5oz) grated mature Cheddar cheese
30g (1oz) grated Parmesan cheese

FOR THE BUTTERED CRUMBS

15g (½oz) butter
30g (1oz) white breadcrumbs
25g (1oz) grated Cheddar cheese

Preheat the oven to 180°C/350°F/gas mark 4.

Bring a large saucepan of water to the boil and add 2 teaspoons of salt. Sprinkle in the macaroni and stir to make sure it doesn't stick together. Cook for 10–15 minutes until just soft. Drain well.

Bring 600ml (1 pint) water to the boil and add 1½ teaspoons of salt. Add the sprouts and cook for 2–3 minutes. Strain and refresh under cold water. Drain well.

Melt the butter in a saucepan. Add the sliced leeks, season with salt and pepper, toss, cover and cook over a gentle heat for 3–4 minutes. Turn off the heat and allow the leeks to continue to cook in the residual heat while you make the sauce.

To make the mornay sauce, melt the butter, add the flour and cook over a medium heat, stirring occasionally, for 1–2 minutes. Remove from the heat. Whisk in the milk gradually; bring back to the boil, stirring all the time. Add the mustard, parsley (if using) and cheese, season with salt and pepper to taste. Add the cooked macaroni, bring back to the boil and season to taste.

To assemble, spread one-third of the macaroni in the base of a 30 x 20.5 x 6cm (12 x 8 x 2½in) gratin dish. Top with the well-drained sprouts, another third of macaroni, then the leeks (add the juices to the remaining sauce) and spread the remaining macaroni evenly over the top.

To make the buttered crumbs, melt the butter, turn off the heat, add the breadcrumbs and leave to cool. Stir through the grated cheese and sprinkle evenly over the gratin. Cook for 15–20 minutes until golden on top and bubbling. Flash under a grill for a few minutes if necessary. Serve with a green salad.

ROAST CAULIFLOWER STEAKS WITH GINGER & SPICES

Roasting is a brilliant way to cook cauliflower and you can serve it plain or embellish it in lots of exciting ways. This dish is terrific as a vegan or vegetarian main course. Think of it as a base for lots of tasty toppings: rosemary oil with diced tomato, tapenade with olive oil and rosemary, chermoula, labneh (page 113) with harissa and coriander, pomegranate seeds, tahini, coriander...

SERVES 6 OR MORE **Ve**
1 fresh cauliflower (700g/1½lb)
1 teaspoon grated fresh ginger
1 garlic clove, crushed
1 teaspoon ground cumin
1 teaspoon ground coriander
½ teaspoon ground turmeric
½ teaspoon salt
7 tablespoons extra virgin olive oil
fresh coriander leaves and lemon wedges, to serve

Preheat the oven to 230°C/450°F/gas mark 8.

Remove the leaves from the cauliflower, but just barely trim the base of the core. Cut the cauliflower head into 2cm-(¾in-)thick slices or 'steaks' through the base, save the two outer pieces for a roast vegetable gratin (page 74).

Mix the ginger, garlic, spices and salt with 5 tablespoons of the extra virgin olive oil.

Heat the remaining olive oil in a wide frying pan over a high heat. Sear the cauliflower steaks for about 2 minutes on each side until nicely coloured – use more oil if necessary.

Carefully transfer to a roasting tin in a single layer, spoon the spicy oil over each cauliflower steak, flip over and drizzle a little more on the other side. Roast for 10–15 minutes until the cauliflower feels tender when the stalk end is pierced with the tip of a knife. Check after 8–10 minutes as they may need to be turned.

Serve along with lots of fresh coriander and lemon wedges or as an accompaniment to a simple roast, lamb chop or curry.

MY FAVOURITE LENTIL BURGERS

A good veggie burger recipe is a must in your repertoire – here's one based on lentils. The minimum amount of breadcrumbs results in a deliciously soft burger, the maximum produces a firmer burger, still good but perhaps a little less tasty.

MAKES 8 BURGERS / SERVES 4–8

2 tablespoons extra virgin olive oil
1 large onion, finely chopped (175g/6oz)
1 garlic clove, crushed
225g (8oz) carrots, finely chopped
1 celery stick, finely chopped
1 chilli, deseeded and finely chopped
225g (8oz) Puy or green lentils, boiled for
    approx. 20 minutes, then drained
1½ teaspoons ground cumin
2 teaspoons ground coriander
6 tablespoons chopped flat-leaf parsley and
    coriander or a mixture of fresh herbs,
    such as parsley, coriander, chives, thyme,
    marjoram and tarragon
1 tablespoon lemon juice
1 organic, free-range egg, beaten
50–110g (2–4oz) white breadcrumbs
seasoned plain flour
extra virgin olive oil, for shallow-frying
sea salt and freshly ground black pepper

FOR THE CUCUMBER & MINT RAITA
¼ medium cucumber
½ tablespoon finely chopped onion
1 tablespoon chopped coriander leaves or
    ½ tablespoon parsley and ½ tablespoon mint
150g (5oz) natural yogurt
½ teaspoon cumin seeds

TO SERVE (optional)
Herb mayonnaise (page 35)
chunky homemade chips (page 88)
a tomato salad and/or green salad (pages 34 and 32)

Heat the oil in a frying pan and sauté the onion, garlic, carrots, celery and chilli for 10–12 minutes over a gentle heat until softened and lightly browned. Add the lentils, spices, herbs, lemon juice and seasoning and cook for 5 minutes. Put the lentil mixture into a food processor, add the beaten egg and breadcrumbs and whizz until it holds together but still has a coarse texture. Transfer to a mixing bowl.

Line a baking tray with bakign parchment. Dip your hands in cold water. Shape the lentil mixture into eight burgers, dip in seasoned flour and place on the baking tray. Cover and chill for 30 minutes.

Meanwhile, make the raita. Peel the cucumber if you prefer, cut in half and remove the seeds then cut into 5mm (¼in) dice. Put this into a bowl with the onion, sprinkle with salt and allow to degorge for 5–10 minutes. Drain, and add the chopped coriander or parsley and mint and the yogurt. Toast the cumin seeds, crush lightly and add to the raita. Season. Chill before serving.

Heat 1 tablespoon of oil in a frying pan over a medium heat. Cook the burgers in batches for 3–4 minutes on each side. Drain on kitchen paper. Serve with raita or a herb mayonnaise, maybe some chunky homemade chips, a tomato salad and/or green salad.

SEASONAL VEGETABLE & PANEER CURRY

This vegetable curry is definitely a winner, even determined carnivores can't get enough of this deliciously spiced dish. It's also an excellent base for other additions such as chunks of cooked potato, squash, broccoli, parsnip, carrots or cauliflower florets.

SERVES 4–6 Ⓥ

2 large garlic cloves, crushed
2 chillies, deseeded and roughly chopped
zest of 1 lemon or 2 limes
110g (4oz) coarsely chopped coriander, plus extra to serve
60g (2½oz) cashews, toasted and roughly chopped
1½ tablespoons grated fresh ginger
2 rounded teaspoons ground turmeric
2 rounded teaspoons ground cumin
1 teaspoon salt
4 tablespoons extra virgin olive oil
400ml (14fl oz) can coconut milk

500ml (18fl oz) vegetable stock (page 30)
625g pumpkin or sweet potato (500g/18oz after peeling), peeled and cut into 2cm (¾in) dice
275g (10oz) aubergine, cut into approx. 2cm (¾in) dice
250g (9oz) mushrooms, quartered
250g (9oz) paneer, firm tofu or halloumi, cut into approx. 2cm (¾in) dice
225g (8oz) peas
sea salt and freshly ground black pepper
lemon or lime wedges, to serve

Combine the garlic, chillies, citrus zest, coriander, cashews, ginger, turmeric, cumin and 1 teaspoon of salt in a food processor and whizz to a chunky or smooth purée, depending on your preference.

Heat the olive oil in a large saucepan over a medium heat, stir in the garlic and ginger purée and cook for 3–4 minutes, stirring. Whisk in the coconut milk and stock, bring to the boil and simmer for 8–10 minutes.

Add the chunks of pumpkin or sweet potato and return to the boil. Cover and simmer for 12–15 minutes. Add the aubergine and mushrooms and bring back to the

boil, then cover and simmer for a further 10 minutes. Add the paneer and peas and simmer for a further 3–5 minutes, uncovered, until all of the vegetables are cooked through. Add a little more stock if necessary.

Season with salt and pepper, and squeeze over a little lemon or lime juice, to taste. Sprinkle with lots of coriander and serve with lemon or lime wedges on the side.

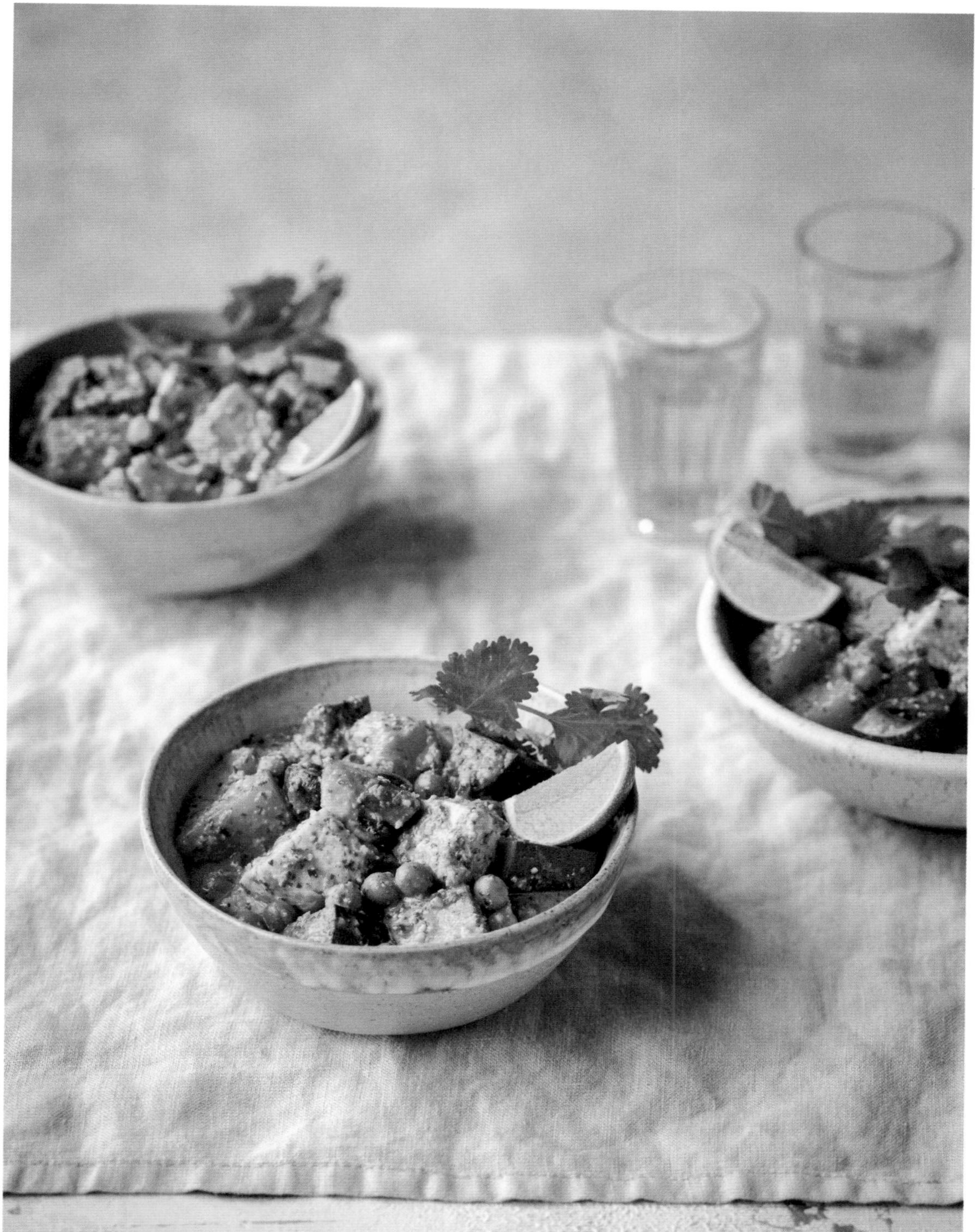

QUESADILLA FOLDIES

These foldies are a hybrid of tacos and quesadillas. Choose three complementary fillings from the suggestions below, plus a chilli sauce. These can be vegetarian or add some sliced meat as well as the melty cheese, if you like.

SERVES 1

1 organic, free-range egg

1 wheat tortilla per person

a handful of mixed grated mozzarella, Gruyére or Parmesan cheese

olive oil, for frying

flaky sea salt and freshly ground black pepper

FILLINGS (optional)

Tomato fondue with chilli & coriander (page 27)

Piperonata (page 26)

Spiced aubergines (page 29)

Refried beans (page 29)

sautéed herby mushrooms

hot chilli or sweet chilli sauce of your choice

thin slices of salami, prosciutto, serrano, cooked ham

FOR THE GUACAMOLE (optional)

1 ripe avocado (Hass if available)

1–2 tablespoons freshly squeezed lime juice

1 tablespoon olive oil

1 tablespoon freshly chopped coriander or flat-leaf parsley

FOR THE TOMATO & CORIANDER SALSA (optional)

4 very ripe tomatoes, chopped

1 tablespoon red or white onion, chopped

1 garlic clove, crushed

½–1 jalapeño or serrano chilli, deseeded and finely chopped

1–2 tablespoons chopped coriander

a squeeze of fresh lime juice

sugar

Heat a cast-iron pan over a low-medium heat.

Whisk the egg and pour on to a plate. Season with salt and pepper. Lay a tortilla on top of the beaten egg and cut from 6 o'clock into the centre. Spread a layer of your chosen filling in a triangle between 9 and 12 o'clock. Fold the 6–9 triangle over the filling. Spread a little hot sauce on top. Spread another layer of filling between 12 and 3. Fold over again allowing a little folding space between that and the next triangle. Finally, a layer of mixed grated cheese between 3–6. Fold the tortilla over to make a triangle. Press gently.

Add a little olive oil to the pan. Lift the fan-shaped foldie into the hot pan. Cook for 3 minutes on one side, flip over carefully and cook on the other side until crisp and golden and the cheese is melting. Transfer carefully on to a piece of parchment paper on a plate.

To make the guacamole, scoop out the ripe flesh from the avocado and mash with a fork or in a pestle and mortar. Add the lime juice, olive oil, chopped coriander, salt and pepper to taste. Cover and keep cool until needed. (A little finely diced chilli or tomato may also be added to the guacamole, if you wish.)

To make the salsa, mix all the ingredients together. Season with flaky sea salt, pepper and sugar.

Enjoy the foldies with a dollop of guacamole, salsa or whatever you fancy.

ADD YOUR FILLINGS

FOLD THE FIRST SECTION

FOLD AGAIN

COOK UNTIL CRISP AND GOLDEN

TOFU, VEGETABLE & PEANUT STIR-FRY

Tofu takes on other flavours brilliantly and is loaded with protein. Keep a couple of packs of organic tofu in your fridge to add to salads and stews.

SERVES 6 **Ve**

2 tablespoons dark soy sauce
2 tablespoons rice wine vinegar
1 tablespoon light soft brown sugar or
   palm sugar
1 teaspoon freshly grated ginger
1 chilli, chopped, or 1 teaspoon chilli flakes
2 teaspoons Chinese five-spice powder
350g (12oz) firm tofu
500g (18oz) Thai fragrant rice
2 tablespoons extra virgin olive oil
200g (7oz) chestnut mushrooms, sliced

1 large red pepper, quartered and sliced at an angle
1 large yellow pepper, quartered and sliced
   at an angle
200g (7oz) broccoli, romanesco or cauliflower
   florets, blanched and refreshed
1 tablespoon toasted sesame oil
50g (2oz) roasted peanuts
2–4 spring onions, sliced
1 tablespoon toasted sesame seeds
flaky sea salt and freshly ground black pepper

Mix the soy sauce, vinegar, sugar, ginger, chilli and five-spice powder together. Pat the block of tofu dry with kitchen paper. Cut the tofu 2.5cm (1in) cubes. Transfer to a small pie dish, cover with the marinade and leave to soak up the flavours for 1–2 hours if time allows. It will be OK left in a cool place in the kitchen but can be popped into the fridge if desired.

Measure the rice in a measuring jug. Wash gently in 2–3 changes of cold water. The final water should almost be clear. Drain the rice well in a sieve or fine strainer, then tip it into a heavy-bottomed saucepan. Add equal volume of water and ½–1 teaspoon of salt. Stir to mix. Bring to the boil, then reduce the heat to the absolute minimum, use a heat diffuser mat if available. Cover with a tight-fitting lid – no steam must escape. Steam the rice for 15–20 minutes, remove from the heat and rest for 5 minutes. The rice will now be dry and fluffy but will keep warm for up to 30 minutes.

Meanwhile, drain the tofu, reserving the marinade. Heat a wok or frying pan, add most of the oil. Cook the tofu in batches for 2–3 minutes on each side until golden, then transfer to a plate. Increase the heat, add the remaining oil, toss the mushrooms and season with salt and pepper. Toss for 5–6 minutes until fully cooked through. Add the peppers, stir and fry for a minute or two, then add the blanched florets. Drizzle with sesame oil and stir-fry for 2–3 minutes. Add the tofu, peanuts, spring onions and the reserved marinade. Allow to bubble and season. Scatter with sesame seeds and serve immediately with the Thai fragrant rice.

BAKED POTATOES WITH GOOD THINGS

Baked potatoes are a brilliant catch-all for lots of yummy toppings including Spiced aubergines or Tomato fondue.

....

SERVES 6 Ⓥⓔ

6 large maincrop potatoes, such as Golden Wonders or Kerr's Pinks
topping of your choice

....

Preheat the oven to 250°C/500°F/gas mark 10.

Scrub the skins of the potatoes well. Prick each potato several times with the tip of a sharp knife. This allows the steam to escape so they don't explode in the oven. Arrange the potatoes on a baking tray, allowing a little space between each one. Bake for 30–50 minutes, depending on size, until fully cooked through. Serve as they are or cut a cross on top and pinch from underneath to open out like a 'flower' to accommodate the topping of your choice.

Meanwhile, prepare your chosen topping. Toppings can be as simple as a sprinkling of grated cheese and chopped spring onions or chives, maybe a few little lardons of crispy bacon or pancetta, a poached egg, or see the suggestions below.

....

GOOD THINGS WITH BAKED POTATOES

✳ **Miso, spring onion & parsley butter**
Melt 50g (2oz) butter, add 1 tablespoon of sliced green spring onions, 1 tablespoon of flat-leaf parsley and 1 tablespoon of white miso. Spoon over the baked potato.

✳ **Smoked fish & horseradish cream** Top with diced smoked mackerel, salmon or trout, some horseradish cream (page 129)and lots of fresh dill.

✳ **Soured cream, lime & paprika** Top with a dollop of soured cream, some freshly grated lime zest and a drizzle of paprika oil (page 100).

✳ **Tomato, mozzarella & basil** Top with some Piperonata (page 26) or Tomato fondue (page 27) with mozzarella and fresh basil leaves.

✳ **Mushroom à la crème** Top with Mushroom à la crème (page 28) with shavings of Parmesan and/or some diced chorizo.

✳ **Lamb breast with tomato salsa & aioli** Serve alongside the Lamb breast (page 157) instead of the rustic roasties.

✳ **Indian-ish baked potatoes** Mix 3 tablespoons of extra virgin olive oil, a couple of teaspoons of freshly grated ginger, 2 tablespoons of diced red onion (washed in cold water), 1 deseeded and finely chopped green chilli and 1–2 teaspoons of chaat or garam masala together in a bowl. Put a dollop of natural yogurt, soured cream or labneh (page 113) on top of each baked potato. Drizzle with the Indian-ish topping, add a few sprigs of coriander and a few flakes of sea salt. Serve.

✳ **Baked sweet potatoes** Don't forget that sweet baked potatoes are also delicious and can be baked in the same way. I love them with a dollop of creamy labneh (page 113), chilli flakes, chunky sliced spring onions and a few flakes of sea salt and freshly ground black pepper. Paprika oil (page 100), Aleppo pepper or a dollop of harissa also work well.

CHEESY POTATO WEDGES

A brilliant cheap and cheerful supper. Sweet potato or even pumpkin wedges are also quick, easy and super nutritious and once again terrifically versatile (see Variations).

....

SERVES 6–8 **V** if using Cheddar cheese

1kg (2¼lb) old potatoes, such as Golden Wonders or Kerr's Pinks
110–175g (4–6oz) grated Cheddar cheese or a mixture of Cheddar, Parmesan and Gruyère
2–4 spring onions, thinly sliced
flaky sea salt and freshly ground black pepper

....

Preheat the oven to 230°C/450°F/gas mark 8.

Roast the potatoes in for 30–45 minutes, depending on size. Sprinkle the grated cheese generously over the potatoes. Pop back into the hot oven or under a hot grill for 5–6 minutes until the cheese has melted.

Sprinkle with sea salt and serve in a hot terracotta dish scattered with the spring onions.

....

VARIATIONS

✳ Garam masala wedges Sprinkle freshly cooked potato wedges with garam masala and a little flaky sea salt. Toss well and season to taste.

✳ Sweet potato wedges (Serves 4) Preheat the oven to 200°C/400°F/gas mark 6. Wash 2 sweet potatoes (approx. 450g/1lb) and cut them into quarters lengthways. Pop into a bowl and drizzle with 2 tablespoons of extra virgin olive oil, then scatter over 1 tablespoon of chopped rosemary or thyme leaves or 1–2 teaspoons of freshly toasted ground cumin and coriander. Season with sea salt and toss into a roasting tin. Bake for 10–15 minutes, turning once, until completely tender and lightly golden. These make a really tasty snack topped with a blob of labneh (page 113), then sprinkled with slivers of pickled red chilli and a few coriander leaves.

✳ Rustic roasties (Serves 4–6) Preheat the oven to 230°C/450°F/gas mark 8. Scrub 6 large 'old' potatoes e.g., Golden Wonders or Kerr's Pinks well (don't bother to peel). Cut into quarters lengthways or cut into 2cm-(¾in-)thick rounds. Put into a roasting tin, drizzle with olive oil (or beef dripping, duck or goose fat if not vegetarian or vegan) and toss so they are barely coated. Roast for 15–30 minutes, depending on size. Sprinkle with sea salt and serve in a hot terracotta dish.

✳ Rustic roasties with soured cream & sweet chilli sauce Serve the rustic roasties in deep bowls with sweet chilli sauce and soured cream – filling and simply delicious.

✳ Rustic roasties with rosemary, thyme, sage or bay Add ½–2 tablespoons of coarsely chopped rosemary or thyme or crushed sage or whole bay leaves with the olive oil and proceed as above.

✳ Rustic roasties with cumin or smoked paprika Mix 1–2 teaspoons of ground cumin or smoked paprika with 110ml (4fl oz) extra virgin olive oil. Toss the potatoes in enough flavoured oil to coat and cook as above. Don't forget the salt.

✳ Spicy rustic roasties Mix 1 teaspoon of curry powder with 110ml (4fl oz) extra virgin olive oil. Toss the potatoes in enough spicy oil to coat them and cook as above. Don't forget the salt.

HOMEMADE CHIPS

It seems we have forgotten how easy it is to make chips at home. What's the secret? Good potatoes, good oil or fat. The variety of potatoes really matters, choose 'old, maincrop' potatoes rather than 'new' potatoes that tend to go limp and soapy inside when fried. Maris Piper or King Edwards are the chippers' favourites. Arran Victory also produce delicious chips. I love Golden Wonder and Kerr's Pink, too.

SERVES 4 Ve

500g–1kg (18oz–2¼lb) maincrop potatoes

Scrub the potatoes well and peel or leave unpeeled according to taste. Cut into similar-sized chips so they cook evenly.

Straw potatoes: finest possible strips about 6.5cm (2½in) long.
Matchstick: similar length but slightly thicker.
Mignonette: Frites, 5mm (¼in) thick x 6.5cm (2½in) long, blanch first at 180°C (350°F) then finish at 190°C (375°F).
Pont Neuf: about 1cm (½in) thick and 6.5cm (2½in) long.
Jumbo chips: about 2cm (¾in) thick and 6.5cm (2½in) long.
Buffalo chips: similar size to Jumbo but unpeeled.

Before cooking, rinse quickly in cold water but don't soak. Dry meticulously with a damp tea towel or kitchen paper before cooking otherwise the water will boil on contact with the oil and may cause it to overflow.

Careful not to overload the basket of the deep-fat fryer or pan, otherwise the temperature of the oil will be lowered, and the chips will be greasy rather than crisp. Shake the pan once or twice, to separate the chips while cooking. Larger chips will need to be cooked twice. To cook the first two types: Fry quickly at 190°C (375°F) for 3–5 minutes until completely crisp.

To cook the last three sizes: Fry twice, once at 160°C (325°F) until they are soft and just beginning to brown. The time will vary from 4–10 minutes depending on size. Drain, increase the heat to 190°C (375°F) and cook for a further 1–2 minutes or until crisp and golden. Shake the basket, drain well, toss on to kitchen paper, sprinkle with a little salt, turn into a hot serving dish and serve immediately.

VARIATIONS

✱ **Thrice-cooked chips** A brilliant way to use up leftover boiled potatoes or cook the potatoes in boiling salted water until almost fully cooked. Drain and cut into peeled or unpeeled chips to desired size. Heat dripping or good-quality oil to 160°C (325°F) in a deep fat-fryer. Cook the chips in batches until golden. Drain well. To serve, heat the oil to 190°C (375°F) and fry once more until crisp and a deep golden colour. Shake the basket, drain well, toss on to kitchen paper, sprinkle with a little flaky sea salt, turn into a hot serving dish and serve immediately.

✱ **Zero-waste potato skin crisps** Scrub the potatoes. Peel using a swivel-top peeler, dry the peels and fry for 5–6 minutes until crisp. Sprinkle with salt and a little smoked paprika if you fancy – a delicious snack.

✱ **Garlic crisps** Cook the crisps as above, put into a hot serving dish, melt some Garlic butter (page 37) and drizzle over the crisps, serve immediately as a snack or as an accompaniment to burgers or steaks.

✱ **Volcanic crisps** Add 1–2 tablespoons of chilli flakes to the butter with the garlic and parsley. Serve as above.

GRATIN DAUPHINOIS

Everyone loves a dish of bubbling gratin Dauphinois, rich and delicious. It's wonderful served with rich meats, perhaps a rib of beef, haunch of venison or steak. Although a classic gratin Dauphinois certainly doesn't have any bits and bobs added to it, it doesn't hurt to occasionally add a few leftover cooked shrimp, flakes of smoked mackerel or salmon, chorizo, pancetta, duck confit or little crispy bits of pork for a supper in one dish.

SERVES 6 Ⓥ

900g (2lb) maincrop potatoes, such as Golden
    Wonders or Kerr's Pinks
250ml (9fl oz) whole milk
250ml (9fl oz) double cream
1 small garlic clove, crushed
freshly grated nutmeg
sea salt and freshly ground black pepper

Choose equal-sized potatoes and slice them into rounds, 5mm (¼in) thick. Don't wash them but dab them dry with a cloth. Spread out on the worktop and season generously with salt and pepper, toss with your hands.

Pour the milk into a heavy-bottomed saucepan, add the potatoes, bring to the boil. Cover, reduce the heat, simmer gently for 10 minutes but keep an eye on the pan so they don't catch on the base.

Preheat the oven at 200°C/400°F/gas mark 6.

Add the cream, garlic and a generous grating of nutmeg to the saucepan. Simmer for a further 20 minutes, stirring occasionally, so the potatoes do not stick to the base. As soon as the potatoes are cooked, take them out with a slotted spoon and put them into a 20.5cm (8in) square gratin dish or six small ovenproof dishes. Pour the creamy liquid over them. Heat or reheat in a bain-marie (page 100) in the oven for 10–20 minutes until bubbly and golden on top.

VARIATIONS

✳ **Gratin Lyonnais** Sweat about 350g (12oz) sliced onions in a little butter. Put a layer of onions between two layers of potato before cooking.

✳ **Gratin Savoyard** Sprinkle 50g (2oz) grated Gruyère and Parmesan cheese or a mature hard cheese over the gratin before baking.

✳ **Cashel Blue cheese & rosemary gratin** Omit the garlic in the recipe above and instead sprinkle about 110g (4oz) crumbled Cashel or Crozier Blue cheese (or Gorgonzola, Roquefort or Stilton) between two layers of potato. If you like, sprinkle 1 tablespoon of freshly chopped rosemary over the cheese before topping up with potatoes.

✳ **Potato, rosemary, thyme & bay leaf gratin** Preheat the oven to 200°C/400°F/gas mark 6. Pour 600ml (1 pint) double cream and 600ml (1 pint) whole milk into a heavy-bottomed saucepan, add 2 crushed bay leaves, 4 sprigs of finely chopped rosemary and some thyme leaves and season with salt and pepper. Bring to the shivery stage over a medium heat, then set aside to infuse. Meanwhile, peel and slice 8 medium potatoes (1.8kg/4lb) into 5mm-(¼in-) thick slices. Rinse the potatoes, then add to the liquid with 5 crushed garlic cloves. Bring to the boil for 4–5 minutes. Transfer to a buttered 30 x 20 x 5cm (12 x 8 x 2in) gratin dish, cover with baking parchment and bake for 45 minutes–1 hour. Uncover and brown in the oven or under the grill before serving.

POTATO, MUSHROOM & LEEK GRATIN

A gorgeous combination – the leeks don't need to be fully cooked before adding to this gratin. If you have a few wild mushrooms, maybe chanterelles or field mushrooms, mix them with ordinary mushrooms for this. If you can find flat ones, all the better. This is also delicious without the leeks and terrifically good with a pan-grilled lamb chop, a steak or as part of a roast dinner.

....

SERVES 8–10 **V** if using Cheddar cheese

25g (1oz) butter, plus extra for greasing
350g (12oz) leeks (prepared weight), sliced into
    5mm (¼in) rounds
1kg (2¼lb) 'old' potatoes, such as Golden Wonders or
    Kerr's Pinks, sliced into 5mm (¼in) slices
1 garlic clove, finely chopped

300g (10oz) mushrooms, such as button,
    chestnut or flat mushrooms, or a
    mixture of cultivated mushrooms,
    oyster mushrooms, shiitake, and enoki, sliced
350ml (12fl oz) single cream
25g (1oz) grated Parmesan (Parmigiano Reggiano) or
    mature Cheddar cheese
sea salt and freshly ground black pepper

....

Preheat the oven to 180°C/350°F/gas mark 4.

Melt the butter in a heavy casserole; when it foams, add the sliced leeks and toss gently to coat with butter. Season with salt and pepper. Cover with baking parchment and a close-fitting lid. Reduce the heat and cook very gently for 3–4 minutes or until semi-soft and moist. Turn off the heat and leave to cook in the residual heat. (The leeks can also be cooked in the oven at 160°C/325°F/gas mark 3 for 10–12 minutes if that is more convenient.) Leeks cooked in this way are delicious as a vegetable on their own.

Bring a large saucepan of water to the boil. Add the potato slices to the boiling water. As soon as the water returns to the boil, drain the potatoes. Refresh under cold water. Drain again and arrange on kitchen paper or a clean tea towel.

Grease a shallow 25.5 x 21.5cm (10 x 8½in) gratin dish or two 12.5 x 19.5cm (5 x 7½in) gratin dishes generously with butter and sprinkle the garlic over the top. Arrange half the potatoes in the bottom of the dish(es) and season with salt and pepper. Spread a layer of half-cooked leeks on top.

Cover with the sliced mushrooms. Season again and finish off with a final layer of overlapping potatoes. (The gratin dish should be full to the top.)

Bring the cream almost to boiling point and pour over the potatoes. Sprinkle the cheese on top and bake for 1 hour until the gratin becomes crisp and golden brown with the cream bubbling up around the edges.

MASHED POTATO

Who doesn't love a big bowl of mashed potato? Comfort food at its very best and an essential accompaniment to so many dishes. If the potatoes are not peeled and mashed while hot and if the boiling milk is not added immediately, the potato will be lumpy and gluey. A potato ricer is guaranteed to produce a light, fluffy mash but the hot, peeled potatoes can also be mashed in a food mixer, adding hot milk and butter or extra virgin olive oil.

SERVES 4 Ⓥ

1kg (2¼lb) unpeeled potatoes, preferably Golden Wonders or Kerr's Pinks
approx. 300ml (10fl oz) whole milk
1 organic, free-range egg (optional)
25–50g (1–2oz) butter
sea salt and freshly ground black pepper

Scrub the potatoes well. Put them into a saucepan of cold water, add a generous pinch of salt and bring to the boil. When the potatoes are about half-cooked, about 15 minutes for 'old' potatoes, strain off two-thirds of the water, replace the lid on the saucepan, put over a gentle heat and allow the potatoes to steam until they are cooked. Peel immediately by just pulling off the skins, so you have as little waste as possible, mash well. (If you have a large quantity, put the potatoes into the bowl of a food mixer and beat with the paddle attachment.)

Meanwhile, bring the milk to the boil. Add the egg (if using) to the hot mashed potatoes and add enough boiling milk to mix to a softish consistency, then beat in the amount of butter you like. Taste and season with salt and pepper.

VARIATIONS

✱ **Fresh herb mash** Fold 4 tablespoons of freshly chopped herbs, such as flat-leaf parsley, chives, tarragon, lemon balm or lovage to the mash.

✱ **Mustard mash** Add 2 tablespoons of English or Dijon mustard and/or 1 tablespoon of wholegrain mustard with 1–2 tablespoons of chopped flat-leaf parsley to the mash.

✱ **Buttermilk & spring onion smashed potatoes** Add 300ml (10fl oz) buttermilk, 25–50g (1–2oz) butter, lots of salt and pepper to the mash. Add 4 finely sliced spring onions, if you like.

✱ **Celeriac & parsnip mash** (Serves 6) Cook 450g (1lb) celeriac, cut into 1cm (½in) cubes, and 350g (12oz) parsnips, cut into 1cm cubes, separately in boiling salted water until soft. Strain both, mash together and add 50g (2oz) butter, season well with salt and pepper and scatter with chopped parsley.

✱ **Colcannon** (Serves 8–10) Scrub 1.8kg (4lb) maincrop potatoes, such as Golden Wonders or Kerr's Pinks, put them in a saucepan of cold water, add a good pinch of salt and bring to the boil. When they are about half-cooked, about 15 minutes, strain off two-thirds of the water, replace the lid on the saucepan, put over a gentle heat and allow the potatoes to steam until they are cooked. Remove the leaves from 225–450g (8oz–1lb) kale or Savoy cabbage. Cook in boiling salted water until soft. Drain, season with salt, pepper and a little butter. When the potatoes are just cooked, bring 450ml (16fl oz) whole milk to the boil. Peel the potatoes and mash quickly while they are still warm, then beat in enough boiling milk to make a fluffy purée. Stir in the kale. Season to taste. Serve immediately in a hot dish with 50g (2oz) butter in the centre. Colcannon can be prepared ahead up to this point, covered and reheated in the oven at 180°C/gas mark 4 for 20–25 minutes.

EGGS, DAIRY

SOFT-BOILED EGGS

The simplest of breakfasts or suppers, a couple of boiled eggs provides a delicious and satisfying meal. Beautiful fresh eggs, boiled gently to perfection, are a true gourmet experience. The albumens (whites) will be tender and slightly 'curdy', the yolks still soft and silky. Eggs are an amazingly nutritious food – incredibly inexpensive considering their nutritive value – high in protein, vitamins and mineral and essential fatty acids.

SERVES 1 Ⓥ

2 fresh, organic, free-range eggs, at room temperature
Brown soda bread (page 22)
best-quality butter
sea salt and freshly ground black pepper

GOOD THINGS WITH SOFT-BOILED EGGS

✱ During asparagus season, use freshly cooked spears to dip into the runny yolks – decadent and delicious.

✱ Spread Marmite or Anchovy butter (page 37) on white toast dippers.

TOP TIP ✱ Eat boiled eggs with a stainless-steel teaspoon as silver or silver-plate cutlery will react with the egg and give it a nasty taste.

Bring a small saucepan of water to the boil, add a little salt and gently slide in the eggs – they must be covered with boiling water.

Bring the water back to the boil and simmer gently for 4–6 minutes, according to your taste. A 4-minute egg will be still quite soft, 5 minutes will almost set the white while the yolk will still be runny and 6 minutes will produce a boiled egg with a soft yolk and solid white.

Meanwhile, slice the soda bread and spread with butter. Then cut into fingers.

Immediately after the eggs are cooked, pop them into egg cups on large side plates and cut the tops open or they will continue to cook. Serve with the soldiers on the side and a pepper mill and sea salt so you can season to taste.

HARD-BOILED EGGS

Hard-boiled eggs are the basis of many delicious snacks or indeed full-blown suppers such as a spicy egg curry (page 105). It may sound counter-intuitive but choose eggs that are a few days old because very fresh eggs are a nightmare to peel. It's best to have the eggs at room temperature before sliding them carefully into well-salted water – the shells are porous, so the flavour will be enhanced by the salt. If the eggs are straight from the fridge, they may crack when they come into contact with the boiling water. Time them accurately – overcooking causes that dark ring around the yolk. Drop them into cold running water to stop them cooking and peel when cool. Hard-boiled eggs will keep for a day or two in the fridge.

organic, free-range hen, duck or guinea fowl eggs

Bring a small saucepan of well-salted water to the boil, gently slide in the eggs, bring back to the boil and simmer for 8–10 minutes according to your taste (12–14 minutes for duck eggs). For jammy eggs with a softish yolk, cook for just 7 minutes. Drain and then cool under cold running water before peeling when cooled.

A LITTLE SECRET ✱ When I travel, I'm never without a little phial of sea salt mixed with Aleppo pepper to sprinkle over hard-boiled eggs at breakfast!

GOOD THINGS TO DO WITH HARD-BOILED EGGS

✱ **Devilled eggs** Split the eggs in half lengthways. Mix the yolks with a little mayonnaise (page 35) and a few finely chopped chives. Spoon into the centre of the whites and decorate with a chive or a sprig of chervil. Chopped anchovies or olives, or sieved Ballymaloe relish are also delicious added to the yolks.

✱ **Oeufs mimosa** Remove the yolks, sieve and mix most of them with mayonnaise. Put a couple of cooked prawns into the cavities. Top with the egg and mayonnaise mix. Coat with a light mayonnaise, sprinkle with some reserved egg yolk. Garnish with chervil. A piece of smoked salmon or mackerel instead of prawns is also good.

✱ **Egg sandwiches** Coarsely chop the peeled eggs, season with salt and pepper and mix with mayonnaise (page 35) and finely chopped chives. Add a little smoked paprika if you fancy.

✱ **Hard-boiled egg salads** Have fun creating hard-boiled egg salad combinations; try the traditional Irish high tea favourite with butterhead lettuce, quartered tomato, pickled beetroot, cucumber, a spring onion and radish. Lay the eggs on a bed of rocket or mixed organic salad leaves, add slices of chorizo and drizzle with mayonnaise and harissa. Try pairing them with smoked mackerel or any warm smoked fish of your choice, pickled beetroot, horseradish mayonnaise and a few chunks of avocado.

✱ **Breakfast scone** Split a freshly baked buttermilk scone in half, butter both sides, add ½ cooked streaky bacon rasher, top with ½ hard-boiled egg, a dollop of relish, any mayonnaise and another rasher of bacon. Top with the other half of the scone and secure with a satay stick.

PERFECT POACHED EGGS

Lots of people are anxious about poaching eggs and if the eggs are stale, it is certainly quite a challenge. But if you have a really fresh egg laid by a happy hen then no fancy egg poachers or moulds are required. Tips about putting vinegar in the cooking water are really only valid for eggs that aren't so fresh – if you have a fresh, organic egg, the albumen is strong enough to hold together.

If you're having friends over, you can poach eggs ahead of time and then reheat them when required. Just cook them for a minute less initially, and then slip them into a bowl of cold water to stop them cooking further. Reheat gently for a minute or two in boiling water until hot through to serve.

SERVES 1 Ⓥ

2 really fresh, organic, free-range eggs
a couple of slices of bread
a knob of butter
sea salt and freshly ground black pepper

Bring a small saucepan of water to the boil. Reduce the heat to a simmer, crack each egg into a cup, swirl the water and slip the egg gently into the whirlpool in the centre. This avoids burning the tips of your fingers as you drop the eggs into the water. The water should not boil again but bubble very gently just below boiling point. Cook for 3–4 minutes until the whites are set and the yolks are still soft and runny.

Meanwhile, toast the sliced bread. Butter and pop it on to a hot plate. Lift out the poached eggs using a perforated spoon; drain and place on top of the toast.

GOOD THINGS TO ENJOY WITH POACHED EGGS

✱ **Eggs Benedict** Lay a slice of cooked ham or a couple of slices of hot crispy bacon on a toasted bun. Top with a freshly poached egg. Coat with Hollandaise sauce (page 36).

✱ **Gilbir Turkish eggs** Add 1 crushed garlic clove to 150g (5oz) natural yogurt. Melt 30g (1oz) butter in a small pan; when it begins to foam add 2 teaspoons of paprika or smoked paprika and stir for 30 seconds. Top the poached eggs with the garlic yogurt, paprika butter and 4–6 shredded mint leaves. Serve immediately with some Turkish bread or toast.

✱ **Eggs Florentine** Serve the poached eggs on a bed of creamed spinach or kale on sourdough toast, drizzle with extra virgin olive oil and sprinkle with Aleppo pepper.

✱ **Poached eggs piperonata** Pop a couple of poached eggs on a bed of hot Piperonata (page 26), season with sea salt and fresh basil leaves.

✱ **Poached eggs, avocado toast & bacon** Pop a freshly poached egg on avocado toast with 2 pieces of cooked streaky bacon.

✱ **Poached eggs with crispy sage** Cook 5–6 sage leaves in a knob of butter until crisp and spoon the sage butter and crispy leaves over poached (or fried) eggs.

✱ **Poached eggs with harissa** Drizzle the poached eggs with 1–2 tablespoons of harissa or smoked paprika oil (page 100).

✱ **Spicy poached eggs** Sprinkle poached eggs with Aleppo pepper, Piment d'Espelette or chilli flakes mixed with chopped flat-leaf parsley.

BAKED EGGS

This dish can be a starter or a snack and there are infinite variations on the theme but the eggs must be super fresh and the cream rich. Although the classic French version always has cream, you can omit the cream if you wish and drizzle with extra virgin olive oil instead.

SERVES 2–4 Ⓥ

15g (½oz) butter
6–8 tablespoons double cream
4–8 fresh, organic, free-range eggs
flaky sea salt and freshly ground black pepper

Lightly butter four 8cm (3¼in) ovenproof ramekins. Heat the cream in a small saucepan over a low heat; when it is hot, spoon about 1 tablespoon into each ramekin and break an egg into the cream. Season with salt and pepper. Spoon the remaining cream over the top of the eggs. Place the ramekins in a container half-filled with boiling water, known as a bain-marie, cover with a lid and bring to a simmer on the hob. Continue to cook gently on the hob or transfer to an oven preheated to 180°C/350°F/gas mark 4 for about 10 minutes for soft eggs and 12 minutes for medium eggs. Serve immediately.

SPECIAL TREAT ✷ If perchance you happen to have a fresh truffle, add a few thin shavings for a feast.

✷ **Baked eggs with ham & cheese** Put 1 tablespoon of chopped cooked ham into each ramekin. Sprinkle ½–1 tablespoon of finely grated Parmesan, Gruyère, Cheddar cheese or a mixture on top of each egg. Bake, covered, as in the main recipe. Omit the ham for a veggie version.

✷ **Baked eggs with smoked fish** Put 1 tablespoon of chopped smoked salmon or flaked smoked mackerel or eel into each ramekin. Add 1–2 tablespoons of chopped flat-leaf parsley to the cream and proceed as in the basic recipe.

✷ **Baked eggs with fresh herbs & Dijon mustard** Mix 2 teaspoons of Dijon mustard and 3 tablespoons of chopped flat-leaf parsley, tarragon, chives and chervil into the cream and proceed as in the basic recipe.

✷ **Baked eggs with yogurt & paprika oil** Top each egg with a dollop of natural yogurt just before serving. Gently heat 1 teaspoon of sweet or smoked paprika in 4 tablespoons of extra virgin olive oil and drizzle over the top.

✷ **Baked eggs with tomato fondue** Put 1 tablespoon of Tomato or Tomato & chilli fondue (page 27) into the base of each ramekin. Bake as in the main recipe, with or without the cheese (see Baked eggs with ham & cheese).

✷ **Baked eggs with Piperonata** Put 1 tablespoon of Piperonata (page 26) into the base of each ramekin. Spoon 1 tablespoon of cream over each egg. Sprinkle ½–1 tablespoon of finely grated cheese on top of each egg; a little cooked bacon, pancetta or diced chorizo may also be added. Bake, uncovered, as in the main recipe.

✷ **Baked eggs with truffle oil** Add 2–3 drops of truffle oil to the cream and proceed as in the main recipe.

BAKED EGGS WITH HAM & CHEESE

BAKED EGGS WITH SMOKED FISH

BAKED EGGS WITH FRESH HERBS

BAKED EGGS WITH YOGURT & PAPRIKA OIL

SCRAMBLED EGGS

Scrambled eggs are a universal favourite, an essential technique and one of the great convertibles – made in minutes from ingredients you probably have in your cupboards or fridge. You need really fresh eggs for gorgeous soft, creamy curds. Here's the tip: start in a cold saucepan. It seems to have become common practice to put the eggs into a hot pan, which results in tough eggs if you're not careful.

SERVES 2 Ⓥ

4 fresh, organic, free-range eggs
2 tablespoons whole milk
a knob of butter
sea salt and freshly ground black pepper
hot buttered toast or soda bread, to serve

Break the eggs into a bowl, add the milk and season with salt and pepper. Whisk until the whites and yolks are well mixed.

Put the butter into a cold saucepan over a low heat, pour in the eggs and scrape the mixture backwards and forwards on the base of the pan (no flipping or rolling), preferably with a flat-bottomed wooden spoon, until the eggs have scrambled into soft creamy curds.

Serve immediately on warm plates with lots of hot buttered toast or fresh soda bread.

Really great scrambled eggs need no further embellishment. Having said that, see opposite for some great additions and accompaniments.

GOOD THINGS WITH SCRAMBLED EGGS

✱ **Green eggs & ham** Add 2–3 tablespoons of chopped chervil to the eggs and serve with 2 slices of ham on hot buttered toast.

✱ **Indian scrambled eggs** Sweat 50g (2oz) chopped onion in olive oil, add 2 very ripe diced tomatoes, ½ teaspoon of grated ginger, ½–1 finely chopped green chilli, ⅛ teaspoon of turmeric and 2 teaspoons of ground cumin. Cook for 3–4 minutes over a medium heat, add 6 beaten eggs and 1 tablespoon of chopped coriander, season and scramble as in the basic recipe.

✱ **Thai scrambled eggs** Add 1 tablespoon of sliced spring onions (or garlic chives), 1–2 teaspoons of fish sauce and 1–2 teaspoons of light soy sauce and scramble as in the basic recipe.

✱ **Vietnamese scrambled eggs** Add 1 tablespoon of sliced spring onions, 1 teaspoon of grated ginger, 2 very ripe diced tomatoes and 1–2 teaspoons of fish sauce to the beaten eggs and scramble as in basic recipe.

✱ **Mexican scrambled eggs** Sweat 60g (2½oz) finely chopped onion and 1–3 finely chopped jalapeños in a little olive oil for 3–4 minutes. Add with 2 very ripe diced tomatoes to 8 beaten eggs. Season, scramble and add lots of fresh coriander at the end of cooking. Serve with warm corn tortillas.

✱ **Greek strapatsada** Add 1 tablespoon of chopped marjoram or oregano and 2 tablespoons of Tomato fondue (page 27) to the beaten eggs, scramble as in the basic recipe, sprinkle with crumbled feta and flat-leaf parsley. Serve with warm pitta bread.

CLASSIC PARMESAN & GRUYÉRE SOUFFLÉ

Guests are always wildly impressed by a well-risen soufflé and it's not rocket science, so don't imagine that you can't do it. A soufflé is simply a well-flavoured sauce enriched with egg yolks and lightened with stiffly beaten egg whites. Soufflés are much more good-humoured than you think and can even be frozen when they are ready for the oven and baked from frozen for a few minutes longer than the timings in the recipe below. I love to make this dish with some of the best Farmhouse cheese too, such as a mature Coolea or Templegall.

SERVES 8–10

45g (1½oz) butter, plus melted butter for greasing the moulds
65g (2½oz) freshly grated Parmesan cheese
25g (1oz) flour
300ml (10fl oz) whole milk

4 organic, free-range eggs
50g (2oz) Gruyère cheese, finely grated
a pinch of cayenne pepper
freshly grated nutmeg
sea salt and freshly ground black pepper

First prepare the soufflé dish or dishes. You can use eight individual soufflé dishes, measuring 7cm (2¾in) in diameter and 4cm (1½in) high or one 15cm (6in) dish, 6cm (2½in) high. Brush the dish(es) evenly with melted butter and dust with 15g (½oz) grated Parmesan.

Preheat the oven to 200°C/400°F/gas mark 6 and place a baking tray in the oven. Melt the butter in a heavy-bottomed saucepan, stir in the flour and cook over a gentle heat for 2–3 minutes. Remove from the heat and whisk in the milk, return to the heat and whisk as it comes to the boil. Then reduce the heat and simmer gently for 3–4 minutes. Remove from the heat.

Separate the eggs and put the whites into a large copper, glass or stainless-steel bowl, making sure it's spotlessly clean and dry. Whisk the yolks into the white sauce one by one, add the grated cheeses, season with salt, pepper, cayenne and a little freshly grated nutmeg. It should taste highly seasoned at this stage because the egg whites will dull the seasoning. Stir over a gentle

heat for a few seconds until the cheeses melt. Remove from the heat. (The soufflé(s) can be made ahead up to this point and refrigerated for several hours.)

Whisk the egg whites with a small pinch of salt, slowly at first and then faster until they are light and voluminous and hold a stiff peak when you lift up the whisk. Stir a few tablespoons into the cheese mixture to lighten it and then carefully fold in the remainder with a thin spatula or long-handled spoon. Pour the mixture into the prepared soufflé dish(es). Bake the individual soufflés for 8–9 minutes or the large one for 20–25 minutes. For the large soufflé, cook in a bain-marie (page 100) and reduce the oven temperature to 180°C/350°F/gas mark 4 after 15 minutes.

Serve immediately followed by a salad of organic leaves. Alternatively, just before the soufflés are cooked, toss a mixture of salad leaves and divide between the plates. Turn a hot soufflé out on to each one and serve immediately with the salad alongside.

INDIAN EGG CURRY

Another must-have recipe, I sometimes add 2–3 diced cooked potatoes to the sauce to make an even more substantial meal. Egg curry is a favourite dish in local dhabas all around India. This spicy tomato sauce makes an irresistible base for the hard-boiled eggs. There are many recipes but this is a South Indian version.

....

SERVES 4–6 **V**

2 tablespoons vegetable or extra virgin olive oil
½ teaspoon mustard seeds
½ teaspoon cumin seeds
½ teaspoon coriander seeds
¼ teaspoon fennel seeds
160g (5¾oz) onion, roughly chopped
½–1 red chilli, chopped
1 teaspoon grated fresh ginger

400g (14oz) can of chopped tomatoes
a pinch of sugar
200ml (7fl oz) coconut milk
3 tablespoons chickpea (gram) flour
3 teaspoons curry powder
6–8 hard-boiled eggs (page 98)
2–3 cooked potatoes, diced (optional)
sea salt and freshly ground black pepper
a handful of fresh coriander leaves, to garnish

....

Heat the oil in a sauté pan over a medium heat and add the mustard, cumin and coriander seeds. When the mustard seeds start to pop, add the fennel seeds, stir, and add the onion, chilli and ginger. Cover and cook for 4–5 minutes until the onion is soft but not coloured. Add the chopped tomatoes, season with salt and pepper and the sugar and continue to cook for 5–8 minutes.

Meanwhile, whisk 110ml (4fl oz) water with the coconut milk, chickpea flour, curry powder and a generous teaspoon of salt. Add to the pan, bring to the boil and continue to cook for 15–20 minutes until the sauce has mellowed and thickened. Taste and adjust the seasoning as necessary. Add the hard-boiled eggs and potatoes, if using, and heat through over a gentle heat for 3–4 minutes.

Serve scattered with the coriander leaves.

HUEVOS RANCHEROS

You will need a small to medium frying pan with a lid for this classic Mexican breakfast dish. You can top with fried eggs instead of adding the eggs to the sauce and I love a blob of Guacamole (page 82) or a couple of avocado slices as an accompaniment. Black beans (page 67) transform it into an even more substantial breakfast or brunch dish.

SERVES 2

1 tablespoon extra virgin olive oil
25g (1oz) fresh (uncured) chorizo, diced
½ onion, chopped (170g/6oz)
1 small red chilli, thinly sliced
½ medium red pepper, diced into 1cm (½in) pieces (approx. 125g/4½oz)
200g (7oz) canned chopped tomatoes
a good pinch of sugar
1 heaped tablespoon chopped coriander, plus ½ tablespoon to garnish
2 organic, free-range eggs
flaky sea salt and freshly ground black pepper

TO SERVE (optional)

warm corn tortillas
grated Cheddar or Oaxacan cheese
sliced avocado or Guacamole (page 82)
black beans (page 67)

Add the oil to a 19cm (7½in) frying pan over a low heat and fry the chorizo for a few minutes until the fat has been released. Increase the heat to medium, then add the onion, chilli and pepper and continue to fry for 5–8 minutes.

Add the chopped tomatoes, season with salt, pepper and the sugar. Add the coriander, reduce the heat and simmer for 8–10 minutes until the spicy tomato sauce thickens somewhat.

Make two indentations in the sauce and break an egg into each one. Season with a little salt and pepper. Place a lid on the pan and continue to cook over low-moderate heat for 4–5 minutes until the eggs are cooked to your liking. Sprinkle with the chopped coriander.

If you would prefer to serve with fried eggs, heat a couple of tablespoons of extra virgin olive oil in a frying pan over a medium heat. Crack in the eggs and fry for 3–4 minutes until the whites are set but the yolks are still soft and runny.

Put the pan on the table and serve with warm corn tortillas (an essential accompaniment), grated cheese, avocado and/or black beans as you wish.

FLEXIBLE FRITTATA

A frittata is cooked slowly over a very low heat, during which time you can be whipping up a delicious salad to accompany it. This basic recipe is flavoured with grated cheese and a generous sprinkling of herbs. Like an omelette, you'll occasionally want to add some tasty morsels to ring the changes. Perhaps some spinach, chard, asparagus, broad beans, smoked mackerel, chorizo, 'nduja, cherry tomatoes, roast squash or pumpkin, or cauliflower or broccoli florets. The list is endless but be careful you don't use it as a dustbin – think about the combination of flavours before you empty your fridge. Individual frittatas can be made in muffin tins or in a small pan for a feast for two or double the quantities below and use a larger 25cm (10in) pan to feed 6–8. Leftovers are also delicious tucked into a baguette with a few salad leaves.

SERVES 3–4

5 large, organic, free-range eggs
½ teaspoon salt and lots of freshly ground
    black pepper
1 tablespoon chopped flat-leaf parsley
1 teaspoon thyme leaves

1 tablespoon chopped basil or marjoram
40g (1½oz) Gruyére cheese, grated
15g (½oz) Parmesan or Pecorino cheese, grated
15g (½oz) butter
salad of your choice (page 32), to serve (optional)

Whisk the eggs well in a bowl, season with the salt and some freshly ground black pepper. Add the chopped fresh herbs and grated cheeses.

Melt the butter in a 15cm (6in) non-stick frying pan over a medium heat. When the butter starts to foam, tip in the eggs. Cook for 3–4 minutes.

There are two cooking methods:
1. As soon as the edges have set, transfer to an oven preheated to 170°C/325°F/gas mark 3 and cook for 15–20 minutes until just set.
2. Alternatively, as soon as the edges are set, reduce the heat under the pan to as low as it will go. Leave the eggs to cook gently for 12 minutes on a heat diffuser mat or until the underneath is set. The top should still be slightly runny. Preheat the grill. Pop the pan under the grill for 1 minute to set but not brown the surface.

Slide a palette knife under the frittata to free it from the pan. Slide on to a warm plate. Serve cut into wedges with salad of your choice.

GOOD THINGS TO ADD TO FRITTATA

✳ **Smoked salmon & goat's cheese**
Add 110–175g (4–6oz) smoked salmon to the beaten eggs and replace the herbs with dill. Dot 110g (4oz) goat's cheese on top before cooking.

✳ **Asparagus, rocket & wild garlic** Add 150g (5oz) blanched asparagus tips, a handful of rocket and 4 tablespoons of chopped wild garlic leaves to the beaten eggs.

✳ **Chilli & coriander** Add ½–1 diced red chilli to the beaten eggs and replace the herbs with 1 tablespoon of chopped coriander.

MUSHROOM & THYME LEAF TART

Everyone loves this flavoursome tart, one of the few tarts that tastes super warm or cold. Small (15cm/6in) mushroom tarts cooked for 15 minutes may be served straight from the oven as appetizers. Omit the pastry for a pastry-less quiche.

SERVES 6

15g (½oz) butter

1 tablespoon extra virgin olive oil

300g (10½oz) mushrooms, chestnut or flat mushrooms if possible, roughly sliced

1 teaspoon fresh thyme leaves

225ml (8fl oz) double cream

2 organic, free-range eggs, plus 1 egg yolk

50g (2oz) freshly grated Parmesan cheese, preferably Parmigiano Reggiano

a good pinch of cayenne pepper

sea salt and freshly ground black pepper

FOR THE RICH SHORTCRUST PASTRY

115g (4oz) plain flour

50-75g (2-3oz) cold butter

1 organic, free-range egg or egg yolk, plus a little beaten egg white

First, make the shortcrust pastry. Sift the flour into a wide bowl, cut the butter into cubes and rub into the flour across your fingertips. Keep everything as cool as possible; if the butter is allowed to melt, the finished pastry may be tough. When the mixture looks like coarse breadcrumbs, stop. Whisk the egg or egg yolk and add about 1 tablespoon of water. Take a fork or knife (whichever you feel most comfortable with), and add just enough liquid to bring the pastry together, then discard the fork and collect the dough into a ball with your hands. This way you can judge more accurately if you need a few more drops of liquid. Although slightly damp pastry can be easier to handle and roll out, the resulting crust will be tough and may well shrink out of shape as the water evaporates in the oven. Drier and more difficult -to-handle pastry will give a crispier, shorter crust.

Wrap the pastry in baking parchment and leave to rest in the fridge for a minimum of 15-30 minutes. This will make the pastry much less elastic and easier to roll.

Roll out the pastry thinly and use it to line a 18cm (7in) tart tin with a pop-up base; the pastry should come up just above the top of the tin. Trim off the excess, leaving a slight overhang. Line with baking parchment and fill with dried beans. Rest in the fridge for 15 minutes.

Preheat the oven to 180°C/350°F/gas mark 4.

Bake the pastry case 'blind' for about 25 minutes (page 112). The base should be almost fully cooked. Remove the baking parchment and beans. Brush the base with a little beaten egg white and cook for 3-4 minutes. This will seal the base and avoid the 'soggy bottom' effect.

Meanwhile, melt the butter in a frying pan over a very high heat, add the oil and fry the mushrooms for 5-6 minutes. Add the thyme leaves and season with salt and pepper. Cook until all the juice has evaporated and set aside to cool.

Whisk the cream in a bowl with the eggs and egg yolk, then stir in the cooled mushrooms and Parmesan cheese. Add the cayenne and more seasoning if necessary. Pour into the pre-baked pastry case and bake for 30-40 minutes or until the filling is set and the top is delicately browned.

Serve with a good green salad (page 32), if you wish.

QUICHE LORRAINE

What pops into your mind when you hear the word quiche? A pastry shell with a savoury custard filling? For me, there are myriad variations on the theme, but if I had to choose just one it would be this Quiche Lorraine, named after the Lorraine region of north-east France. When it's carefully made and properly seasoned, you realize why it's become a much-loved classic.

Look on this basic pastry shell, egg and cream mixture as a master recipe. Flavourings can be added to the savoury custard, such as roast or cooked vegetables – pumpkin, goat's cheese and rocket or chorizo can be arranged on the base of the pastry case as can prawns or shrimps.

SERVES 6–8

1 x quantity rich shortcrust pastry (page 110)
1 tablespoon extra virgin olive oil
175g (6oz) smoked or unsmoked streaky bacon, cut into 1cm (½in) lardons
100g (3½oz) chopped onions
3 organic, free-range eggs and 2 egg yolks
300ml (10fl oz) double cream

1 scant tablespoon chopped flat-leaf parsley
1 scant tablespoon chopped chives
110g (4oz) freshly grated Gruyère cheese or 75g (3oz) freshly grated Gruyère and 25g (1oz) freshly grated Parmesan cheese
sea salt and freshly ground black pepper
green salad (page 32), to serve (optional)

Preheat the oven to 180°C/350°F/gas mark 4.

Line a 23cm (9in) tart tin with a pop-up base with the pastry. Line with baking parchment and fill to the top with dried beans. Rest in the fridge for 15 minutes and then 'bake blind' for about 25 minutes. The base should be almost fully cooked. Remove the baking parchment and beans. Brush the base and insides with a little beaten egg white and bake for 3–4 minutes. This will seal the base and avoid the 'soggy bottom' effect.

Heat the oil in a sauté pan over a medium heat and cook the bacon for 4–5 minutes until almost crisp. Remove to a plate and leave to cool. Add the chopped onions to the pan, cover and sweat gently over a low heat in the same oil (and bacon fat) for 8–10 minutes.

Meanwhile, whisk the eggs in a medium bowl, add the cream, herbs, cheese, cooled bacon and onions. Mix

well and season with salt and pepper. Taste or heat a frying pan over a gentle heat and cook a teaspoon of the mixture for 2–3 minutes until it coagulates – taste and correct the seasoning if necessary.

Pour the filling into the pre-baked pastry case – it should come to the top. Bake for 30–40 minutes or until the centre has just set. Test by putting a skewer or the tip of a knife into the centre. It will come out clean when the quiche is cooked. Serve warm with a green salad or some salad leaves and relish.

GOOD TO KNOW ✳ Always sweat the onions, peppers, mushrooms, etc before adding to a quiche, otherwise they are likely to be underdone when the custard is set. The oven temperature should not go above 180°C/350°F/gas mark 4 to stop the filling scrambling.

GOOD THINGS WITH LABNEH

✱ Labneh with wild garlic or summer herbs
Add 2 tablespoons of finely chopped wild garlic or chervil, chives, thyme, flat-leaf parsley or tarragon to the labneh, taste and add a little salt and honey if necessary. Pile into a bowl, strain and drip for 30 minutes. Transfer to a bowl and scatter with wild garlic flowers, if available. Serve with crackers.

✱ Labneh on sourdough toast with chargrilled lamb, pomegranate & mint Pile sliced chargrilled lamb on to a slice of toasted sourdough. Sprinkle with a few pomegranate seeds and some shredded mint. Serve with a dollop of labneh.

✱ Roast carrots with labneh, pistachios & watercress (Serves 4) Roast 500g (18oz) quartered carrots drizzled with4 tablespoons of extra virgin olive oil, 1 teaspoon of ground cumin, 1 teaspoon of ground coriander and ½ teaspoon of Aleppo pepper at 200°C/400°F/gas mark 6 for 10–15 minutes until caramelized at the edges. Serve on a bed of labneh with pistachios and watercress sprinkled over the top.

✱ Labneh with pomegranate, mint & pistachios
Sprinkle a few pomegranate seeds and coarsely chopped pistachios over the labneh and top with shredded mint.

✱ Shrikhand (Serves 8-10) Put a square of muslin into a bowl. Pour in 2kg (4½lb) labneh or Greek yogurt, tie the ends and leave to drip overnight. Transfer to a clean bowl. Infuse a generous pinch of saffron strands in 1 tablespoon of warm water. Stir every last drop into the yogurt. Mix in ¼ teaspoon of roughly crushed green cardamom seeds and 175g (6oz) caster sugar. Turn into a serving dish. Chill. Sprinkle with 2 tablespoons of coarsely chopped pistachios and serve.

LABNEH — SOFT YOGURT CHEESE

Labneh is so fun and easy to make. It's simply dripped yogurt that results in a thick, deliciously smooth, soft 'cheese'. Your friends will be mightily impressed if you produce it for a dinner party. Labneh is an easy way to dabble in 'cheesemaking' and can be used for sweet or savoury dishes, added to salads or enjoyed with berries, nuts, dates or figs. It's the base for many good things including shrikhand, one of my favourite Indian desserts.

Use full-fat yogurt for a creamier result – it can be cow's, sheep's or goat's milk. You can also start with a top-quality commercial natural yogurt.

MAKES APPROX. 500G (18OZ) LABNEH, depending on the quality of the yogurt **V**
1kg (2¼lb) whole-milk yogurt (unsweetened)

Line a strainer with a double thickness of sterilized muslin or cheesecloth (if you don't have either, then a light, clean cotton tote bag works brilliantly). Place it over a bowl. Pour in the yogurt. Tie the four corners of the cheesecloth together to make a loose bundle and suspend over the bowl. Leave it in a cool place to drip for 4–8 hours depending on the quality of the yogurt – Jersey milk yogurt can take as little as 2 hours. Remove the cheesecloth, put the labneh into a clean bowl (wash the cloth and save for another batch).

Use immediately or chill until needed, preferably in a covered glass bowl. Stir in a little softly whipped cream to soften if necessary or perhaps a little runny honey to sweeten.

FISH, SEAFOOD

PAN-GRILLED MACKEREL WITH MISO

A spanking-fresh mackerel is my absolute favourite sea fish. I cook it in myriad ways, including roasted and poached, but do try this recipe as it's astonishing how the miso enhances the flavour. Other fish such as haddock or hake may also be used but it's particularly good with mackerel.

SERVES 2

2 tablespoons white miso
½ tablespoon runny honey
1 teaspoon Asian sesame oil
1 teaspoon dark soy sauce
4 fresh mackerel fillets
olive oil, for cooking
green salad (page 32), to serve

Whisk the miso, honey sesame oil and soy sauce together. Coat each mackerel fillet in the marinade and leave for 15–20 minutes to absorb the flavours.

Heat a griddle pan over a medium heat. Wipe any excess marinade from the mackerel. Drizzle with olive oil, then cook, skin-side down, for about 2 minutes.
Flip over to cook the flesh side for a further 2–3 minutes, depending on the thickness of the fish. Serve immediately with a salad of organic leaves.

Alternatively, you can roast the mackerel on a baking tray at 180°C/350°F/gas mark 4 for 5–6 minutes.

BALIK EKMEK — MACKEREL FISH BREAD

At the Eminou end of the Galata bridge in Istanbul, you'll find boats selling balik ekmek, or 'fish bread'. The Turks love mackerel but other fresh fish such as haddock or hake can also be used.

SERVES 6

6 rolls or 4 x 15cm (6in) pieces of baguette
extra virgin olive oil, for cooking the fish
6 fresh mackerel fillets
approx. 1 teaspoon Aleppo pepper or sumac
sea salt and freshly ground black pepper
6–12 leaves of little gem or lollo rosso lettuce
12–18 slices of tomato or Turkish tomato salad (page 34), to serve

FOR THE PARSLEY, CAPER & SPRING ONION MAYONNAISE

1 tablespoon chopped flat-leaf parsley
1 tablespoon chopped spring onions
1 teaspoon chopped baby capers
1 x quantity homemade mayonnaise (page 35)

Heat a griddle pan over a high heat. Split the bread in half and grill on the crumb side for a minute or two until grill-marked. Remove from the pan and set aside.

Lightly oil the mackerel, season with salt, pepper and Aleppo pepper or sumac and reheat the griddle pan over a high heat. When it is hot but not smoking, place the mackerel skin-side down in the pan. Reduce the heat slightly and cook for 4–5 minutes. Turn over and cook for 3–4 minutes until crisp and golden.

Mix the parsley, spring onions, capers and mayonnaise together and spread a little on the bread. Top each piece with a mackerel fillet, 2–3 slices of tomato or some tomato salad, a leaf or two of lettuce and serve.

BAKED FLAT FISH WITH HERB BUTTER

My mother-in-law, Myrtle Allen, taught me how to cook fish in this way. The following master recipe can be used for a variety of fresh, flat fish including plaice, Dover sole, lemon sole, brill, turbot, halibut, flounder or megrim. Depending on the size of the fish, it can be served as a starter or main course. For a large halibut, brill or turbot, double or triple the amounts listed below..

SERVES 4

4 very fresh plaice, lemon sole or other flat fish on the bone
110g (4oz) butter
4 teaspoons each finely chopped flat-leaf parsley, chives, fennel and thyme leaves
sea salt and freshly ground black pepper

Preheat the oven to 180°C/350°F/gas mark 4.

Turn the fish on its side and remove the head, if you like. Wash the fish and clean the slit by the head very thoroughly. With a sharp knife, cut through the skin around the edge of the fish where the 'fringe' meets the flesh. Be careful to cut neatly and to cross the side cuts at the tail or it will be difficult to remove the skin later.

Sprinkle the skin with salt and pepper and lay it in 1cm (½in) of water in a shallow baking tin or tins. Bake for 20–30 minutes, according to the size of the fish. The water will be almost – but not completely – evaporated when the fish is cooked. If it dries up completely, the fish will stick to the tin. To check whether the fish is cooked, lift the flesh from the bone close to the head where the flesh is thickest; it should lift off the bone easily and be white with no trace of pink.

Just before serving, melt the butter and stir in the freshly chopped herbs. Catch the skin down near the tail and pull it off gently (the skin will tear badly if not properly cut). Lift the fish on to hot plates and spoon some butter over the top. Serve immediately with some extra butter on the side. Sublime.

GOOD THINGS TO ENJOY WITH BAKED FLAT FISH

✱ Roast cherry tomatoes Preheat the oven to 220°C/425°F/gas mark 7. Lay 500g (18oz) cherry tomatoes on the vine on a baking tray, allow 3–4 per person. Drizzle with extra virgin oil, season with salt and pepper and roast for 4–5 minutes until the tomatoes are just about to burst.

✱ Buttered cucumber with fennel Peel and dice 2 cucumbers into 1cm (½in) pieces. Melt 25g (1oz) butter in a heavy-bottomed saucepan or casserole, toss in the cucumber and season with salt and pepper. Cover and sweat over a low heat for about 20 minutes until just soft, stirring occasionally. Add ½ tablespoon of snipped fennel (dill is also delicious). Season to taste.

✱ Simple chard Pull the green leaves off 450g (1lb) chard and wash, drain and coarsely chop the stalks into pieces about 5cm (2in) long. Cook them in boiling salted water for 3–4 minutes until they feel almost tender when pierced with the tip of a knife. Add the leaves, and toss for 2–3 minutes until they are soft and wilted. Drain well. Toss in 25g (1oz) butter or 2–3 tablespoons of olive oil and 1 tablespoon of freshly chopped herbs of your choice – marjoram, rosemary, tarragon or basil are good. Season to taste and serve immediately.

✱ Piperonata (page 26)

✱ Hollandaise sauce (page 36)

FLASH-ROAST FISH

This is a brilliant technique for cooking fish and there are a huge variety of flavoured butters, sauces and salsas (pages 37, 36 and 82) that can be served alongside this master recipe. I've suggested three below: fresh herb butter or oil, nasturtium and parsley butter or hollandaise with mussels, but I also love tomato and coriander salsa, teriyaki sauce and ginger hollandaise.

....

SERVES 6–8 PEOPLE
depending on whether it's being served
as a starter or main course

1kg (2lb 4oz) fresh white fish or wild salmon,
   whole or cut into portions
approx. 2 tablespoons chilli flakes or
   2 tablespoons ground cumin and/or coriander
   or fennel seeds
olive oil or clarified butter (page 15), melted
flaky sea salt and freshly ground black pepper

TO SERVE (optional)
FOR THE FRESH HERB BUTTER OR OIL
50–110g (2–4oz) butter or extra virgin olive oil
4 teaspoons mixed finely chopped fresh flat-leaf
   parsley, chives, fennel and thyme leaves

FOR THE NASTURTIUM BUTTER
110g (4oz) butter
zest of ½ lemon
approx. ½ tablespoon freshly squeezed lemon juice
1 tablespoon chopped flat-leaf parsley
1 teaspoon chopped chives
25 nasturtium flowers, coarsely chopped
4 nasturtium leaves, coarsely chopped

FOR THE MUSSEL HOLLANDAISE (OPTIONAL)
Hollandaise sauce (page 36)
18–24 cooked and shelled mussels

....

Preheat the oven to 240°C/475°F/gas mark 9.

Descale the fish if necessary, fillet and remove the pin bones.

Line a baking tray with baking parchment. Lay the fish on top skin-side down. Brush with extra virgin olive oil or melted clarified butter. Season with flaky sea salt and pepper and/or chilli flakes or other spices of your choice, if using. Roast the fish for 5–10 minutes, depending on the thickness of the fish, until cooked and tender – careful, it's easy to overcook.

Meanwhile, make your chosen accompaniment. To make the fresh herb butter, melt the butter and stir in the freshly chopped herbs. For fresh herb oil, substitute extra virgin olive oil for the butter and stir in the herbs. For the nasturtium and parsley butter, cream the butter, add the lemon zest and beat in the lemon juice bit by bit. Add the parsley, chives and nasturtium flowers. Form into a roll and wrap in greaseproof paper, twist the ends like a cracker and transfer to the fridge to chill until needed.

For the mussel hollandaise, add the mussels to the hollandaise sauce.

Transfer the cooked fish to warm plates. Spoon a little freshly made herb butter or oil or sauce over the top and allow to melt over the fish. Serve immediately.

HOW TO HOT-SMOKE FISH

A brilliant basic skill and so fun to do. You don't need any special equipment – a cookie tin will do. The salt draws out excess moisture and inhibits the growth of bacteria. Both salt and smoke preserve. Once you master the simple technique of hot-smoking, why not try smoking chicken or duck breasts? (See Variations below).

SERVES 4

4–6 portions of wild salmon, haddock, mackerel
or hake
pure salt (not table salt)

TO SERVE

Horseradish sauce (page 129)
Homemade mayo, Dill mayo, Wholegrain mustard
mayo or Mustard & dill mayo (page 35)
Pickled cucumber salad (page 34)

Lay the fish fillets, flesh side up, on a tray and sprinkle with pure salt as though you were seasoning generously. Be careful as it's easy to over-salt if the fillets are thin.

Depending on the thickness of the fish, leave for at least 1 hour but not more than 3 hours. Dry the fillets with kitchen paper, place on a wire rack and leave to dry in a cool, airy place for about 30 minutes. Sprinkle 2 tablespoons of sawdust (I use apple wood) on the base of a rectangular cookie tin or smoking box.

Put a wire rack into the tin and lay the fish, flesh side up, on top. Put the box over a medium gas flame for a minute or so until the sawdust starts to smoulder. Cover the box.

Reduce the heat and smoke for 4–7 minutes depending on the thickness of the fish. Turn off the heat and leave the fish to sit in the tin/smoked unopened for 5 minutes.

Remove from the box and serve with any of the suggestions above or as you fancy.

VARIATIONS

✱ Hot-smoked chicken or duck breasts
Sprinkle 4 organic chicken or duck breasts (weighing about 1kg/2lb 4oz) on both sides with dairy salt. Leave to cure in a fridge for about 30 minutes. Put 2 tablespoons of sawdust on some foil in a cookie tin or hot-smoker. Put it over a high heat until it starts to smoke. Lay the chicken on a wire rack over the sawdust. Put the lid on the smoker (ensure it's a tight fit). Reduce the heat down to low. Hot-smoke for about 15 minutes, depending on the size. Leave to rest for at least 10–12 minutes before eating. The chicken should be fully cooked through. Delicious served warm or cold in salads.

MERMAID'S FISH PIE

This easy-peasy recipe can be used for almost any round fish, including cod, pollock, ling, haddock, salmon or grey mullet. I like to prepare a big batch to make several pies, which can be refrigerated or frozen and reheated another day.
A chopped hard-boiled egg and 110g (4oz) cooked peas add extra nourishment and flavour. Try crispy Cheddar crumbs or croutons for toppings to ring the changes.

SERVES 6–8

1.1kg (2lb 8oz) cod, hake, haddock or grey mullet fillets, or a mixture
15g (½oz) butter, for greasing
600ml (1 pint) whole milk
approx. 20g (¾oz) roux (made by blending 10g/¼oz softened butter with 10g/¼oz plain flour – page 60)
¼ teaspoon Dijon mustard
150–175g (5½–6oz) freshly grated Gruyère or Cheddar cheese or 75g (3oz) freshly grated Parmesan cheese
2 tablespoons chopped flat-leaf parsley
110g (4oz) cooked mussels, shelled

110g (4oz) cooked prawns, peeled
½ can chopped anchovies, approx. 4 fillets (optional)
4 sheets of filo pastry (optional)
melted butter, for brushing
flaky sea salt and freshly ground black pepper

FOR THE MASHED POTATO (optional)

900g (2lb) unpeeled potatoes, preferably Golden Wonders or Kerr's Pinks, scrubbed well
300ml (10fl oz) whole milk
1–2 organic, free-range egg yolks or 1 whole egg and 1 egg yolk
25–50g (1–2oz) butter

If using mashed potato topping, put the potatoes into a saucepan of cold water, add a good pinch of salt and bring to the boil. When the potatoes are about half-cooked after about 15 minutes, strain off two-thirds of the water, replace the lid on the saucepan, put over a gentle heat and steam for 5–6 minutes until cooked. Peel immediately by pulling off the skins, put the potatoes into the bowl of a food mixer and beat or mash by hand.

Bring the milk to the boil. Beat the eggs into the hot mashed potatoes and add enough boiling creamy milk to mix to a soft, light consistency, then beat in the butter, the amount depending on how rich you like your potatoes. Season to taste with salt and pepper.

Preheat the oven to 180°C/350°F/gas mark 4. Skin the fish and cut into 6–8 portions. Season well with salt and pepper. Lay the pieces of fish in a lightly buttered 26cm (10½in) sauté pan and cover with the milk. Bring to the boil, then simmer for 4–5 minutes until the fish has changed from translucent to opaque. Remove the fish to a plate with a slotted spoon.

Bring the milk back to the boil and whisk in enough roux to thicken the sauce to a light coating consistency. Stir in the mustard, cheese and parsley. Season to taste. Add the cooked fish, most of the mussels and prawns and the anchovies, if using, and stir gently to coat with the sauce. Transfer carefully to a serving dish or dishes. Spoon or pipe a layer of mashed potato on top of each one and tuck the reserved prawns and mussels into the potato topping. Alternatively, brush each filo sheet with melted butter and cut into four pieces. Scrunch up each piece of filo pastry and arrange side by side on top of the pie(s).

Bake (both toppings) for 15–20 minutes until bubbling and the filo is crisp and crunchy.

BAJA-STYLE FISH TACOS

All along the coast in Baja, California, the beach shacks offer fish tacos and there's no reason you can't enjoy them at home too. If you'd rather not have batter, you can just sprinkle the fish fillets with a mixture of salt and spices such as cumin, paprika and maybe some chilli powder before shallow frying.

MAKES 10

10 fillets of fresh fish, haddock, monkfish brill, plaice, lemon sole, weighing about 125g (4½oz) each
olive oil, for deep-frying

FOR THE CHILLI BEER BATTER
225g (8oz) plain flour
2 teaspoons English mustard powder
2 teaspoons mild or hot chilli powder
1 teaspoon salt
2 teaspoons granulated sugar
3 organic, free-range eggs
225ml (8fl oz) light beer or beer and water

FOR THE CHIPOTLE MAYONNAISE
225ml (8fl oz) mayonnaise (page 35)
1½ tablespoons puréed chipotle chillies in adobo
juice of 1 lime
1 tablespoon chopped coriander
a pinch of salt

TO SERVE
10 corn tortillas
20 lettuce leaves
Guacamole (page 82) or avocado slices
Tomato salsa (page 82)
a few sprigs of coriander

First make the chilli beer batter. Sift the flour into a bowl and add the mustard and chilli powders, salt and sugar. Make a well in the centre, crack in the eggs, then gradually add the beer, whisking all the time from the centre to the outside of the bowl in ever increasing concentric circles until all the flour is incorporated. Cover and leave to stand while you make the mayonnaise.

Mix the chilli in adobe, lime juice and coriander with the mayonnaise and season to taste.

Warm the corn tortillas either individually in a pan or better still wrap them in a parcel and heat at 180°C/350°F/gas mark 4 for 5–10 minutes.

Heat the oil in a deep-fat fryer to 190°C (375°F). Dip each fish fillet in the batter, then cook for 4–7 minutes until crisp and drain on kitchen paper. This will depend on the thickness of the fish. Alternatively, fry in a deep saucepan with 5–7.5cm (2–3in) depth of olive oil.

Put a little lettuce on one half of a warm tortilla, top with a fillet of crispy fish, some chipotle mayo, guacamole, tomato salsa and a sprig of coriander, fold over and enjoy!

BURMESE FISH CURRY

A simple but totally delicious fish curry taught to me by a wonderful Burmese cook called Nan Win, the chef at the Heritage Restaurant on the edge of Inle Lake – its particularly delicious spicing merits a place in this book and transports me back to Myanmar and its gentle people.

....

SERVES 6

2 tablespoons light extra virgin olive oil
150g (5oz) onion, chopped
1 green chilli, split lengthways
3 garlic cloves, finely chopped or grated
1 teaspoon freshly grated or chopped ginger
1 teaspoon paprika or ½ teaspoon sweet and
   ½ teaspoon smoked paprika
¼ teaspoon ground turmeric
a pinch of sugar

4 ripe tomatoes, peeled and chopped, or
   200g (7oz) canned chopped tomatoes
450g (1lb) monkfish, cod or haddock
2 tablespoons fish sauce
3 whole bird's eye chillies (try increasing this to
   5 or 6 for a more authentic heat)
approx. 2 tablespoons coarsely chopped coriander
sea salt and freshly ground black pepper
Thai fragrant rice or Pilaff rice (pages 85 and 52),
   to serve

....

Heat the oil in a wok, add the onion and chilli and stir-fry over a medium heat for 4–5 minutes until almost soft. Add the garlic, ginger, paprika, turmeric and sugar, stir and cook for a minute. Add the tomatoes and continue to cook for about 5 minutes until the tomatoes are soft and melting.

Meanwhile, cut the fish into 2.5cm (1in) pieces and add to the sauce, plus 100ml (3½fl oz) water if the tomatoes are not juicy enough. Toss gently to coat the fish and cook for 3–5 minutes until it becomes opaque. Add the fish sauce and chillies and continue to cook for 2–3 minutes until the fish is cooked through. Season with pepper and sugar and add more fish sauce rather than salt if it needs it. Add lots of coriander and serve with Thai fragrant or Pilaff rice.

CRAB & BLOOD ORANGE SALAD

I'm fortunate to live close to the little fishing village of Ballycotton in East Cork so I buy crabs whole and we pick the meat ourselves. Frozen crab meat is widely available – it varies in quality so choose the best, most succulent crab meat for this recipe. Pomelo, the pale yellow giant citrus, have a flavour reminiscent of grapes and grapefruit. I enjoyed them all over Myanmar and in salads in Thailand and Vietnam, often combined with shredded chicken or shellfish. Look out for them in the citrus section of your greengrocer.

SERVES 4

3 blood oranges or red or pink grapefruits, segmented, or 1 pomelo, peeled and shredded
300g (10½oz) cooked white crab meat or small cooked shrimps
a handful of dill, roughly chopped
a handful of mint leaves, roughly chopped
a handful of coriander leaves, roughly chopped, stems finely chopped, plus sprigs to garnish
2 banana or 3 Asian shallots, sliced
1 large red chilli, finely sliced
1 bird's eye chilli, finely diced
50g (2oz) roasted peanuts

FOR THE DRESSING

2 Thai chillies, finely sliced
1 large garlic clove, crushed
3 tablespoons caster sugar
4 tablespoons fish sauce
4 tablespoons freshly squeezed lime juice
4 tablespoons rice wine vinegar
3 tablespoons extra virgin olive oil

To make the dressing, put all the ingredients in a screw-top jar and shake well to dissolve the sugar. This dressing is best used fresh but it will keep in the fridge for 2–3 days.

To assemble the salad, cut each blood orange (or grapefruit or pomelo) segment into 2–3 pieces. Combine with the remaining ingredients, except the peanuts, in a wide bowl. Pour over just enough dressing to coat, toss gently, sprinkle with the roasted peanuts and scatter some sprigs of coriander over the top to serve.

If you need to roast the peanuts, preheat the oven to 200°C/400°F/gas mark 6.

Spread the peanuts over a roasting tray, roast for about 7-10 minutes, shaking once or twice. Take the tray outside and blow off the loose skins – it sounds odd but it's exactly what everyone does all over Asia. Return the peanuts to the oven if they are not already golden brown all over.

SARDINES ON WAFFLES

For me, sardines are a must-have in my pantry, but buy carefully. My preference is for hand-caught sardines in extra virgin olive oil but there are lots of options in tomato sauce, smoked or with chilli. The number and the size in a can varies from 2–6, hence 2–3 cans in the ingredients list below.

SERVES 4/MAKES 12 X 15CM (6IN) WAFFLES

1 teaspoon freshly squeezed lemon juice
1 tablespoon extra virgin olive oil
2–3 (approx. 140g/5oz) cans of sardines
4 tablespoons Pickled cucumber salad (page 34)
a piece of fresh horseradish
fresh dill sprigs
sea salt and freshly ground black pepper

FOR THE HORSERADISH & DILL CREAM

3–6 tablespoons freshly grated horseradish
2 teaspoons white wine vinegar
1 teaspoon freshly squeezed lemon juice
¼ teaspoon English mustard powder
1 teaspoon granulated sugar
225ml (8fl oz) softly whipped cream
1–2 tablespoons freshly chopped dill

FOR THE PICKLED ONIONS

125g (4½oz) red onion, sliced into rings
1 tablespoon cider vinegar
1 tablespoon granulated sugar
2 tablespoons spring onions, sliced at an angle
2 handfuls of flat-leaf parsley sprigs

FOR THE WAFFLES

175g (6oz) plain flour
15g (½oz) granulated sugar
2 teaspoons baking powder
350ml (12fl oz) whole milk, slightly warmed
50g (2oz) butter, melted
2 organic, free-range eggs, separated

To make the horseradish and dill cream, put the horseradish in a bowl with the vinegar, lemon juice, mustard powder, ¼ teaspoon of salt, pepper and the sugar. Fold in the cream and dill. Season to taste. It should be thick but pourable. Put the red onions into a bowl, add the vinegar, sugar and a pinch of salt. Stir.

Sift all the dry ingredients for the waffles into a deep bowl with a pinch of salt. Make a well in the centre. Mix the warm milk and melted butter together and whisk in the egg yolks. Pour into the well in the dry ingredients. Stir to form a batter. Whip the eggs whites stiffly and gently fold into the batter.

To make the dressing, whisk the lemon juice with the extra virgin olive oil and season with salt and pepper.

Heat a waffle iron. Pour a 75g (3oz) ladle of batter on to the hot iron and cover with the lid. Cook for 3–4 minutes until crisp and golden. Continue until you've used all of the batter or you've cooked as many waffles as you wish.

Meanwhile, add the spring onions to the red onions and toss together.

Lay a waffle on a warm plate. Drizzle over some horseradish and dill cream. Top with 2–6 sardines, depending on size. Mix a couple of tablespoons of parsley with some of the pickled onions. Add some pickled cucumber and drizzle with a little dressing. Toss and season to taste. Pile roughly over the sardines. Finish with a grating of fresh horseradish, top with a few sprigs of dill and serve as soon as possible.

SALAD NIÇOISE WITH TUNA

In Provence there are many versions of this colourful salad, which makes a wonderful summer lunch. Some include crisp red and green pepper and others omit the potato for a less substantial salad. Use the best tuna and anchovies you can find. Fillets of pan-grilled mackerel are also delicious as an accompaniment to this salad (see Variations below).

....

SERVES APPROX. 8

FOR THE SALAD

8 medium, waxy new potatoes, such as Pink Fir Apple, cooked but still warm
3–4 ripe tomatoes, peeled and quartered
110g (4oz) cooked French beans, topped and tailed and cut into 5cm (2in) lengths, blanched and refreshed
1 dessertspoon chopped chives
1 dessertspoon chopped flat-leaf parsley
1 dessertspoon chopped annual marjoram or thyme
1 crisp lettuce
3 hard-boiled eggs (page 98), shelled and quartered
12 black olives, preferably Niçoise

1 teaspoon capers (optional)
120g (4½oz) can tuna and/or 8–9 canned anchovies
8 tiny spring onions
sea salt, freshly ground black pepper and sugar

FOR THE DRESSING

50ml (2fl oz) white wine vinegar
175ml (6fl oz) extra virgin olive oil
2 large garlic cloves, mashed
½ teaspoon Dijon mustard
1 tablespoon chopped flat-leaf parsley
1 tablespoon chopped basil or annual marjoram

....

Mix all the ingredients for the dressing together with a good pich of salt and pepper – it needs to be very well seasoned otherwise the salad will be bland.

Slice the potatoes into 5mm- (¼in-)thick slices and toss in some dressing while still warm. Season with salt and pepper. Toss the tomatoes and beans in some more dressing, season with salt, pepper and sugar and sprinkle with some of the chopped herbs.

Line a shallow bowl with lettuce leaves. Arrange the rest of the ingredients on top of the potatoes, finishing off with olives, capers, if using, and chunks of tuna and/or the anchovies. Drizzle some more dressing over the top. Sprinkle over the remaining herbs and the spring onions and serve.

VARIATIONS

✳ Salad Niçoise with pan-grilled or barbecued mackerel Dry each mackerel fillet with kitchen paper. Dip in well-seasoned flour. Spread a little soft butter on the flesh side of each fillet as though you were meanly buttering a slice of bread. Preheat a griddle pan or barbecue. Cook the mackerel, flesh side down, for 2–3 minutes, then turn over and cook the skin side for about 2 minutes until the skin is crispy and golden. Serve one or two fillets of mackerel criss-crossed on top of each portion of salad.

✳ Vegetarian salad Niçoise Omit the tuna and/or anchovies and add strips of roasted red and yellow peppers and chargrilled onions instead.

MOULES PROVENÇALE

These garlicky mussels are a perennial favourite and super easy to make. Don't skimp on the garlic or they can taste rather dull and 'bready'. The same quantity of clams, cockles or oysters are also delicious served in this way. Try watercress or wild garlic instead of parsley in the butter.

SERVES 6–8

48 mussels, weighing about 600g (1¼lb)

FOR THE GARLIC BUTTER

2 large garlic cloves
2 tablespoons finely chopped flat-leaf parsley
1 tablespoon olive oil
75g (3oz) butter, softened
approx. 110g (4oz) fresh, white breadcrumbs

Check that all the mussels are closed. If any are open, tap the mussel on a worktop, if it does not close within a few seconds, discard. (The rule with shellfish is always, 'If in doubt, throw it out'.) Scrape any barnacles from the mussel shells (only necessary when wild). Wash the mussels well in several changes of cold water. Then spread them in a single layer in a saucepan, covered with a folded tea towel or a lid and cook over a gentle heat for 2–3 minutes – the mussels are cooked just as soon as the shells open.

Remove them from the pan immediately or they will shrink in size and become tough.

Remove the beard (the little tuft of tough 'hair' which attached the mussel to the rock or rope it grew on). Discard one shell. Loosen the mussel from the other shell but leave it in the shell. Leave them to get quite cold.

Meanwhile, make the garlic butter. Peel and crush the garlic and pound it in a mortar with the parsley and olive oil. Transfer to a food processor and gradually beat in the butter. Spread the soft garlic butter evenly over the mussels in the shells and dip each one into the soft, white breadcrumbs. They may be prepared ahead to this point and frozen in a covered box lined with baking parchment.

Arrange in individual serving dishes. Brown under the grill and serve with crusty white bread to mop up the delicious garlicky juices.

HOW TO MAKE BREADCRUMBS ✱ Save all leftover white bread for breadcrumbs. Cut off the crusts (save for dried crumbs), tear each slice into 3–4 pieces, then drop into a liquidizer or food processor and whizz for 30 seconds–1 minute. Use immediately or freeze in bags to use another time. You can also include the crusts, if you wish. The breadcrumbs will be flecked with lots of crust but these are fine for stuffings and any other dish where the crumbs do not need to be white. Use for breadcrumb stuffings, coating fish or meat and buttered crumbs for gratins.

For dried breadcrumbs, spread the crusts out on a baking tray. Bake in the oven at 100°C/220°F/gas mark ¼ for 2–3 hours. Cool, then liquidize the dried crusts a few at a time into fine breadcrumbs. Sieve and store in a screw-top jar or a plastic box until needed. No need to freeze, they keep for months. Use for coating cheese or fish croquettes.

STIR-FRIED PRAWNS & PORK WITH CRISPY NOODLES

Super-fast and delicious, I love the contrast and textures of sweet, sour, sharp and salty flavours. You can also enjoy this piled into lettuce leaves or wraps.

SERVES 4

100g (3½oz) rice vermicelli
6 tablespoons vegetable oil
4 tablespoons finely chopped shallots
6 garlic cloves, finely sliced
½ –1 teaspoon chilli flakes (or to taste)
400g (14oz) minced pork
200g (7oz) cooked prawns or shrimps, cut into 8mm (⅜in) chunks

a large handful of beansprouts or
   80g (3oz) spring onions, cut at an angle
1–2 tablespoons light soft brown sugar
2 tablespoons fish sauce
2 tablespoons mirin
a large handful of coriander leaves
juice of 2 limes, plus lime wedges to serve

Break the vermicelli into shortish lengths about 10–12.5cm (4–5in).

Deep-fat fryers vary in size so fill the fryer up to the recommended line and heat the oil to 180°C (350°F). Alternatively, fill a deep saucepan with 5–7.5cm (2–3in) depth of oil.

Cook the noodles in batches until crisp – they puff up like magic in just a few seconds. Drain on kitchen paper.

Heat 3cm (1¼in) oil in a wok over the highest heat, add the shallots and stir-fry for 1 minute. Add the garlic, chilli flakes and pork and continue to stir-fry for a further 2 minutes or until the pork is almost cooked. Add the prawns, beansprouts, sugar, fish sauce and mirin and stir-fry for 2–3 minutes or until the prawns are heated through. Add the coriander. Toss, taste and add more fish sauce, mirin or sugar if necessary. Add the lime juice.

Spoon the pork and prawn mixture over the drained noodles. Serve with lime wedges on the side. Alternatively, pile into lettuce leaf wraps.

MEAT, POULTRY

ONE-DISH ROAST CHICKEN SUPPER

THAI RED CHICKEN CURRY WITH
PICKLED VEGETABLES

ROAST CHICKEN & MUSHROOM PIE

ROAST CHICKEN & COUSCOUS SALAD

CHICKEN & BROCCOLI PASTA PIE

SPICY CHICKEN, PEANUT & SPRING
ONION STIR-FRY

CRISPY DUCK LEGS WITH ONIONS & ROSEMARY

PAN-GRILLED DUCK WITH BUTTERED CABBAGE

PORK WITH GENTLE SPICES

A GUTSY BEEF STEW WITH POLENTA

BASIC BEEFBURGERS

BALLYMALOE HOMEMADE SAUSAGES

LAMB MEATBALLS WITH YOGURT & MINT

SLOW-COOKED LAMB BREAST WITH RUSTIC
ROASTIES, AIOLI, TOMATO SALSA & ROCKET

SPICED LAMB PIE

ONE-DISH ROAST CHICKEN SUPPER

Another lip-smackingly delicious dish that family and friends love me to cook for them. A whole roasting tray of crispy chicken, bacon and potatoes, perfumed with rosemary and thyme leaves. For a feistier flavour, substitute one-third to half the bacon for diced chorizo. Halve the quantities below for a smaller serving.

....

SERVES 8–10

2 tablespoons extra virgin olive oil, plus
   extra for drizzling
500g (18oz) streaky bacon lardons
2kg (4½lb) free-range, organic chicken thighs,
   drumsticks and wings
2–3 tablespoons thyme leaves
1–2 tablespoons chopped rosemary

1.1kg (2½lb/about 10 large) potatoes
250g (9oz) onions, sliced
60–110ml (2–4fl oz) hot chicken stock
   (page 30 – optional)
flaky sea salt and freshly ground black pepper
green salad (page 32) or Tomato fondue (page 27)
   or Piperonata (page 26), to serve

....

Preheat the oven to 230°C/450°F/gas mark 8.

Heat the oil in a roasting tin, add the bacon and toss over a high heat until it is beginning to colour. Remove to a plate with a perforated spoon.

Season the chicken generously with salt and pepper. Put into a large bowl and scatter with most of the thyme leaves and chopped rosemary, reserving some for the potatoes. (I sometimes add a sprinkling of chilli flakes or smoked paprika – it gets a brilliant reaction.) Toss well.

Peel the potatoes and cut into 1cm- (½in-)thick chips. Dry and season well with salt, pepper and the reserved herbs. Add to the bowl with chicken. Drizzle with the bacon fat and olive oil from the pan and toss once again.

Scatter the onions and bacon over the base of a 37 x 31cm (14½ x 12½in) roasting tin, or two smaller 30 x 20cm (12 x 8in) tins. Arrange the chicken and potatoes haphazardly on top, making sure that the potatoes are popping up. Drizzle with a little more oil. Roast for 45 minutes–1 hour or until the chicken is cooked through (the juices should be running clear if pricked with a knife) and the chips are crispy at the edges. (Organic chicken pieces are larger, so the cooking time can be up to 1¼ hours.) Add the chicken stock at the end if the dish needs a little more juice.

Serve from the tin, family style, with a good green salad and vegetables of your choice, such as Tomato fondue or Piperonata.

THAI RED CHICKEN CURRY WITH PICKLED VEGETABLES

Red and green Thai curry pastes are brilliant standbys to have in your pantry. Homemade pastes can be hotter and fresher but some of the ingredients can be difficult to source, so good-quality bought versions are a great option to have on hand. Be careful with the chilli if you are not sure how hot you like your curry.

SERVES 6

400ml (14fl oz) can coconut milk, separated into thick and thin (I use Thai Gold)
½–1 tablespoon red Thai curry paste
6 organic skinless chicken breasts (weighing 700g/1½lb in total), cut into bite-sized pieces
6 makrut (kaffir) lime leaves, roughly torn
20 Thai basil leaves, torn
1 tablespoon fish sauce
1 red Thai chilli, deseeded and finely sliced
sea salt and freshly ground black pepper
fresh coriander leaves, to garnish
Thai fragrant rice (page 85), to serve

FOR THE PICKLED VEGETABLES (optional)

150g (5oz) granulated sugar
200ml (7fl oz) rice wine vinegar
1 level teaspoon salt
100g (3½oz) artichokes, cut into matchsticks
100g (3½oz) carrots, cut into matchsticks
50g (2oz) celery, cut into matchsticks
½ cucumber (160g/5¾oz), quartered, excess seeds removed and sliced thinly at an angle (130g/4¾oz deseeded)
6 French breakfast radishes, halved
2 shallots, sliced lengthways
1 red chilli, deseeded and finely sliced

To make the pickled vegetables, mix the sugar, vinegar, salt and 200ml (7fl oz) water together in a small saucepan. Bring to the boil and simmer for 1–2 minutes. Remove from the heat and leave to cool. When cool, pour the pickle over the vegetables and chilli in a Kilner jar, cover and leave to pickle for at least 1 hour. The pickled vegetables keep for up to a month in the fridge, but are best eaten sooner.

Put the thick coconut milk and curry paste into a heavy wok or pan over a high heat, mix and fry until oil begins to rise to the top and the mixture smells cooked. Add the chicken and stir-fry for 3–4 minutes. Add the thin coconut milk, lime leaves, Thai basil and fish sauce and cook for 8–10 minutes. Add the sliced chilli and season to taste.

Scatter the coriander leaves over the top and serve with Thai fragrant rice and the pickled vegetables, if desired.

ROAST CHICKEN & MUSHROOM PIE

Everyone loves a homely chicken pie. Mushroom à la crème makes a perfect base to coat tasty morsels of leftover chicken and ham. Snip in a little tarragon if you have some to hand.

SERVES 6

225–350g (8–12oz) leftover roast chicken (pages 18–19) or a mixture of chicken and ham, cut into bite-sized pieces
2 x quantity Mushroom à la crème (made with half milk and cream – page 28)
150ml (5fl oz) chicken stock (page 30) or whole milk (optional)
1 tablespoon chopped tarragon (optional)
Potato & herb mash (page 93)

Preheat the oven to 180°C/350°F/gas mark 4.

Stir the chicken into the mushroom a la crème. Season to taste. Add a little chicken stock or milk if too rich or a little thick. Snip in a little tarragon, if using. Season to taste. Transfer the filling to a 1.2-litre (2-pint) pie dish or smaller individual dishes. Top with a layer of potato and herb mash. Cook for 15–20 minutes or until hot and bubbling. Flash under a preheated grill to brown the top(s) if necessary. Serve immediately.

Alternatively, top with flaky puff pastry, brush with egg wash and make a hole in the centre. Bake at 230°C/450°F/gas mark 8 for 10-15 minutes, reduce the temperature to 200°C/400°F/gas mark 6 and bake until the pastry is cooked through and the filling is bubbling. Garnish with a sprig of parsley and serve.

ROAST CHICKEN & COUSCOUS SALAD

One of the many delicious ways to use up leftover roast chicken or turkey. Swap out the couscous for freekeh, pearled spelt or orzo.

SERVES 4–6

225–300ml (8–10fl oz) hot chicken stock (page 30) or water
175g (6oz) couscous
600g (1¼lb) leftover roast chicken (pages 18–19)
2 tablespoons pumpkin seeds
2 tablespoons dried cranberries or cherries
2 tablespoons fat sultanas
2 tablespoons pistachios, roughly chopped
sea salt and freshly ground black pepper
2 tablespoons coarsely chopped fresh mint leaves
seeds from 1 pomegranate
extra virgin olive oil, for drizzling
4–6 heaped tablespoons yogurt
pomegranate molasses, for drizzling

Pour the hot stock over the couscous, cover and leave for about 15 minutes until the water is fully absorbed.

Shred the chicken into bite-sized pieces. Put into a mixing bowl with the pumpkin seeds, dried fruit and pistachios. Season generously with salt and pepper and most of the mint leaves and pomegranate seeds.

Drizzle the couscous with extra virgin olive oil and fluff up with a fork. Fold into the other ingredients and season to taste.

Just before serving, divide the salad between plates and top each with a dollop of thick yogurt and a trickle of pomegranate molasses and the reserved mint leaves and pomegranate seeds.

CHICKEN & BROCCOLI PASTA PIE

A super comforting family supper that everyone will love. This works well as a base recipe, so try substituting other tasty morsels such as smoked mackerel or wild salmon. Double the quantities to feed a crowd of family and friends.

....

SERVES 4–5

250g (9oz) broccoli florets
3 organic, free-range eggs
50ml (2fl oz) whole milk
20g (¾oz) finely grated Parmesan cheese
100g (3½oz) freshly grated mature Cheddar cheese
40g (1½oz) cooked crispy bacon, cut into 7mm (⅜in) strips, or 50g (2oz) bacon and 25g (1oz) chorizo, cut into 5mm (¼in) dice
100g (3½oz) leftover roast chicken (pages 18–19), cut into 2cm (¾in) pieces

110g (4oz) cooked al dente macaroni
1½ tablespoons chopped flat-leaf parsley
15g (½oz) freshly grated Parmesan or a mixture of Parmesan and Cheddar cheese
extra virgin olive oil, for brushing
flaky sea salt and freshly ground black pepper
green or tomato salad (pages 32 and 34) or Tomato fondue (page 27), to serve

....

Preheat the oven to 180°C/350°F/gas mark 4.

Blanch and refresh the broccoli in a pan of boiling water for 1–2 minutes. Drain well.

Whisk the eggs and milk together in a bowl. Add the remaining ingredients, season with salt and pepper and mix well. Fry off a spoonful of the mixture in a warm pan to check the seasoning.

Put a 22.5cm (8¾in) cast-iron saucepan over a medium heat. Brush the base and sides generously with extra virgin olive oil. Pour in the macaroni mixture.

Cook for 3–4 minutes until the egg starts to cook on the base and around the edges. Transfer to the oven and bake for about 25 minutes until just set in the centre.

Remove from the oven and leave to sit for 5 minutes, then turn out on to a warm platter. Serve in pie-shaped pieces with a tomato or green salad or some Tomato fondue.

SPICY CHICKEN, PEANUT & SPRING ONION STIR-FRY

We all need a tasty stir-fry in our repertoire, so use this recipe as a base and have fun experimenting with different variations. Try thinly sliced broccoli, romanesco or cauliflower florets instead of or alongside the pepper or 125g (4½oz) sugar snap peas, French beans, peas or thinly sliced asparagus in season. Swap the extra virgin oil for toasted sesame oil, or try adding 2–3 teaspoons of fish sauce or teriyaki sauce or replacing the peanuts with cashews. Make sure the wok is over the highest heat to ensure the vegetables don't stew.

SERVES 6

500g (18oz) egg noodles
3 tablespoons extra virgin olive oil
250g (9oz) organic boneless chicken thighs, sliced into 7mm strips
3 large garlic cloves, crushed or grated
1 teaspoon peeled and grated fresh ginger
200g (7oz) onion, thinly sliced
225g (8oz) red peppers, sliced into 5–7cm (2–2¾in) strips
125g (4½oz) carrots, sliced into 5–7cm (2–2¾in) strips
5 tablespoons dark soy sauce
½–1 teaspoon palm or light soft brown sugar
50g (2oz) roasted and salted peanuts
2 tablespoons spring onions, sliced at an angle
2 tablespoons chopped coriander
sea salt and freshly ground black pepper

Cook the noodles according to the packet instructions. Drain, rinse and set aside.

Heat a wok over the highest heat until smoking. Drizzle a little oil into the wok, swirl, add the chicken. Stir and cook for a couple of minutes until it changes colour and you are happy that it's cooked through. Season well with salt and pepper. Add a little more oil if necessary, followed by the garlic, ginger and onion. Stir-fry for a minute or so over the highest heat. Add the peppers and carrots and continue to toss and cook for a further 3–4 minutes. Add the cooked noodles, soy sauce and sugar and stir-fry for 2–3 minutes. Season to taste, then add the peanuts.

Turn out on to a hot platter, sprinkle with the spring onions and coriander. Enjoy immediately.

CRISPY DUCK LEGS WITH ONIONS & ROSEMARY

Crispy duck legs with melting onions infused with rosemary and duck juices – this is definitely one of my favourite winter suppers and is brilliant for entertaining. I sometimes swap in thyme leaves for the rosemary as both are gutsy, perennial herbs. Serve with potato wedges (page 87) and a salad of winter leaves (page 32).

SERVES 6

6 organic, free-range duck legs
extra virgin olive oil, for frying
2kg (4½lb) medium onions, cut into quarters
    or one-sixth depending on size
2 teaspoons finely chopped rosemary,
    plus whole sprigs to serve
450g (1lb) Jerusalem artichokes, white
    turnips or potatoes, peeled and cut into
    2.5cm (1in) chunks (optional)

60–110ml (2–3¾fl oz) chicken or duck stock
    (page 30 – optional)
flaky sea salt and freshly ground black pepper
potato wedges and a winter salad (pages 87
    and 32), to serve (optional)

Preheat the oven to 240°C/475°F/gas mark 9.

Season the duck legs all over with salt. Heat a tiny drop of oil in a heavy 25cm (10in)/3.2-litre (5½-pint) casserole and cook the duck, skin-side down, for 4–5 minutes over a medium heat until well browned. Turn and brown on the other side for 2–3 minutes.

Remove the duck legs to a plate, increase the heat and fry the onions in batches for 3–4 minutes until lightly golden. Pour off some of the fat if there is an excessive amount. Sprinkle generously with the freshly chopped rosemary and season well with salt and pepper.

Top with the Jerusalem artichokes, turnips or potatoes, if using, and arrange the duck legs on top. Cover with a lid and cook in the oven for about 1 hour or until the duck is cooked through and crisp, and the onions are soft, juicy and slightly caramelized. Check every now and then.

Add a little stock at the end of cooking if you'd like it juicer.

Serve the duck legs with the vegetables and cooking juices, garnished with sprigs of fresh rosemary, with potato wedges and a winter salad alongside, as you wish.

PAN-GRILLED DUCK WITH BUTTERED CABBAGE

The combination of cabbage and duck is delicious and the flavour of this quickly cooked cabbage has been a revelation for many, even determined cabbage haters. Or you can swap the cabbage for one of the other good things to serve with pan-grilled duck (right).

SERVES 4

4 duck breasts (weighing about 1kg/2lb 4oz), free-range if possible
flaky sea salt and freshly ground black pepper
sprigs of coriander or flat-leaf parsley, to garnish

FOR THE BUTTERED CABBAGE

450g (1lb) fresh Savoy cabbage
25g (1oz) butter, plus a knob to serve
1–2 tablespoons caraway seeds (optional)

Trim the duck breasts and season well with salt and pepper. Score the duck fat with a sharp knife. Lay the duck breasts fat-side down in a cold griddle pan. Cook over a low heat for 10–15 minutes or until the fat is crisp and fully cooked. Turn over and cook for 5–6 minutes until tender, juicy and a little pink. Quite a lot of fat will run out and you may need to pour some off the pan (save for roasties, page 87). Leave to rest for 5–6 minutes.

To make the buttered cabbage, remove the tough outer leaves and divide the cabbage into four. Cut out the stalks, then cut each section into fine shreds across the grain. Put 2–3 tablespoons of water into a wide saucepan with the butter and a pinch of salt. Bring to the boil, add the cabbage and toss constantly over a high heat, then cover and cook for 3–4 minutes. Toss again and add some more salt, pepper and the knob of butter plus the caraway seeds, if using.

Divide the cabbage between four hot plates, arrange a crispy duck breast or very thin slices of duck breast on top. Garnish with a sprig of coriander or parsley and serve.

GOOD THINGS TO SERVE WITH PAN-GRILLED DUCK

* **Red cabbage** Remove any damaged outer leaves from 225g (8oz) red cabbage (Red Drummond if possible). Cut into quarters, remove the core and slice the cabbage finely across the grain. Put approx. ½ tablespoon of wine vinegar, 50ml (2fl oz) water, ½ teaspoon of salt and approx. 1 heaped tablespoon of sugar into a cast-iron casserole or stainless-steel saucepan. Add the cabbage and bring it to the boil. Meanwhile, peel and core 225g (8oz) cooking apples (Bramley) and cut into quarters (no smaller). Lay them on top of the cabbage, cover and continue to cook gently for 30–50 minutes until the cabbage is tender. Do not overcook or the colour and flavour will be ruined. Season to taste, adding more sugar if necessary. Stir the apple through the cabbage and serve.

* **Piquant beetroot** Peel 675g (1lb 8oz) cooked beetroot, using rubber gloves for this operation if you are vain! Chop the beetroot flesh into cubes. Melt 15g (½oz) butter in a sauté pan, add the beetroot, toss then add 150–175ml (5–6fl oz) double cream and bubble for a few minutes. Season with salt, pepper and sugar. Taste and add a little lemon juice if necessary. Serve immediately.

* **Rhubarb sauce** Cut 450g (1lb) red rhubarb into 2.5cm (1in) pieces and put it into a stainless-steel saucepan, add 110g (4oz) sugar and toss. Cook for 5–10 minutes until the juice from the rhubarb starts to melt the sugar, then cover the saucepan and put over a gentle heat and cook for 4–5 minutes until soft. Taste and add a little more sugar if necessary. It should not be too sweet but should not cut your throat either. If you have a spoonful of really good redcurrant jelly, stir it in at the end, otherwise leave it out. Serve warm with roast pork or goose as well.

* **Green gooseberry sauce** Top and tail 275g (10oz) fresh, green gooseberries, put into a stainless-steel saucepan, barely cover with approx. 175ml (6fl oz) stock syrup (page 184), bring to the boil and simmer until the fruit bursts. Taste. Stir in a small knob of butter if you like but it is very good without it. Serve with roast pork, goose or pan-grilled mackerel.

* **Marmalade sauce** Put 400–450g (14oz–1lb) Seville orange marmalade into a saucepan. Chop the peel if necessary. Add the freshly squeezed juice of 1 lemon and heat gently, adding a little water if needed to make a pouring consistency.

PORK WITH GENTLE SPICES

Another gem, this quick, easy and tasty recipe is terrific for entertaining some friends. It's also delicious with the same quantity of chicken breasts instead of the pork.

SERVES 4–6

1–2 teaspoons cardamom pods
1 teaspoon coriander seeds
1 teaspoon cumin seeds
25g (1oz) butter
110g (4oz) onions, chopped
2 organic pork fillets (weighing about 1kg/2lb 4oz)
150ml (5fl oz) chicken stock (page 30)
150ml (5fl oz) double cream
sea salt and freshly ground black pepper
4–6 sprigs of flat-leaf parsley or coriander, to garnish
orzo, basmati rice, noodles or new potatoes, to serve

Press the cardamom pods and extract the seeds, then grind them to a fine powder in a pestle and mortar with the coriander and cumin seeds, or use a spice grinder.

Melt the butter in a sauté pan, add the onions, cover and sweat over a gentle heat for 5–6 minutes until soft. Trim the pork fillets of all fat and membrane. Cut into 2cm (¾in) slices, season with salt and pepper, then toss the fillets in the ground spices. Add to the onions and sauté gently for 2–3 minutes. Cover the pan tightly and cook over a gentle heat for 4–5 minutes or until the pork is cooked but still nice and juicy.

Remove the pork to a serving dish and keep warm. Put the sauté pan back over the heat, add the stock and cream and reduce by half. Season to taste, then add the pork back into the sauce and allow to bubble for a minute or two. (The dish may be prepared ahead to this point and can be reheated in a saucepan over a gentle heat.)

Serve in a hot serving dish garnished with the parsley or coriander with orzo, basmati rice, noodles or new potatoes alongside.

A GUTSY BEEF STEW WITH POLENTA

Of all the beef stews I make, this is the favourite. It can be made in large quantities plus it reheats and freezes brilliantly. Gremolata is a fresh-tasting mix of chopped parsley, garlic and lemon zest, which I use to sprinkle over roast or braised meat, pasta or anything pan-grilled. The polenta can be served the moment it's ready or poured into a shallow, well-oiled dish and left to cool. It can then be sliced and chargrilled, pan-grilled, toasted or fried and served with all sorts of toppings. The quality of polenta varies so choose a really good brand. This stew is also lovely with Colcannon (page 93) instead of the polenta.

SERVES 6–8

3 tablespoons extra virgin olive oil
285g (10oz) sliced onions
2 large carrots, cut into 1cm (½in) slices
1.35kg (3lb) well-hung stewing beef or lean flank, trimmed of any excess fat and cut into 4cm (1½in) pieces
1 heaped tablespoon plain flour
150ml (5fl oz) red wine
150ml (5fl oz) beef stock (page 31)
250ml (9fl oz) homemade tomato purée (page 27) or 3–4 tablespoons of concentrated tomato purée mixed with 225ml (8fl oz) water or 400g (14oz) can chopped tomatoes
175g (6oz) sliced mushrooms
1 tablespoon chopped flat-leaf parsley
sea salt and freshly ground black pepper

FOR THE GREMOLATA (optional)

4 tablespoons chopped flat-leaf parsley
1 generous teaspoon grated or finely chopped lemon zest
2 garlic cloves, finely chopped

FOR THE POLENTA (optional)

1 level dessertspoon salt
225g (8oz) coarse polenta (bramata)
110g (4oz) butter
85–110g (3¼–4oz) freshly grated Parmesan cheese

Preheat the oven to 160°C/325°F/gas mark 3.

Heat 1 tablespoon of the oil in a casserole over a gentle heat, add the onions and carrots, cover with a lid and sweat for 10 minutes.

Heat 1 tablespoon of the oil in a frying pan until almost smoking. Sear the beef on all sides, then add to the casserole. Sprinkle the flour over the meat and cook for 1–2 minutes. Add the wine, stock and tomato purée to the frying pan, bring to the boil and then add to the casserole. Season the casserole with salt and pepper, cover and cook in the oven for 2½–3 hours, depending on the cut of meat.

Meanwhile, heat the remaining oil in a pan over a high heat, sauté the mushrooms and add to the casserole with the parsley about 15 minutes before the end of cooking.

To make the polenta, pour 1.7 litres (3 pints) water into a deep, heavy-bottomed saucepan and bring to the boil,

then add the salt and sprinkle in the polenta very slowly, letting it slip gradually through your fingers, whisking all the time (this should take 2–3 minutes). Bring to the boil and when it starts to erupt like a volcano, reduce the heat to the absolute minimum – use a heat diffuser mat if you have one.

Cook for about 40 minutes, stirring regularly. I use a whisk at the beginning but as soon as the polenta comes to the boil I change to a flat-bottomed wooden spoon. (If you stir constantly over a slightly higher heat, the cooking time can be reduced to about 20 minutes but it is more digestible if cooked slowly over a longer period.) The polenta is cooked when it is very thick but not solid and comes away from the sides of the pan as you stir.

As soon as the polenta is cooked, stir in the butter, Parmesan and lots of freshly ground pepper. Taste and add a little more salt if necessary. It should be soft and flowing; if it is a little too stiff, add some boiling water.

Just before you're ready to serve, make the gremolata by mixing all the ingredients together in a small bowl.

Serve the casserole topped with the gremolata, if using, with the polenta, colcannon, mashed potatoes or noodles and a good green salad alongside, as you wish.

GOOD THINGS TO ADD TO BEEF STEW

✱ Stir through 110g (4oz) green or black olives at the end of cooking.

✱ Add 225g (8oz) diced cooked bacon, pickled pork or chorizo a few minutes before the end of cooking.

✱ Add a couple of chopped anchovies a few minutes before the end of cooking.

✱ Add 225g (8oz) whole Agen prunes 10 minutes before the end of cooking.

BASIC BEEFBURGERS

The secret of really good beefburgers is the quality of the mince, it doesn't need to be an expensive cut but it is essential to use freshly minced beef. A small percentage of fat in the mince will make the burgers sweet and juicy – between 20–25 per cent. One or two tablespoons of Worcestershire sauce, ¼ teaspoon of chilli flakes, 1–2 tablespoons of sambal oelek, 2 tablespoons of fish sauce, 1–2 teaspoons of ground cumin or coriander can be added according to your taste but the recipe below gives a delicious basic burger. If you're looking to eat less but better meat, try the variation with mushrooms – you'll never go back...

SERVES 4

15g (½oz) butter or extra virgin olive oil
75g (3oz) onions, finely chopped (optional)
450g (1lb) freshly minced beef – flank, chump or shin would be perfect
½ teaspoon fresh thyme leaves
½ teaspoon finely chopped flat-leaf parsley
sea salt and freshly ground black pepper
olive oil

TO SERVE (optional)

burger or brioche buns
lettuce
sliced ripe tomatoes
sliced red onion
crispy bacon
avocado slices or a dollop of Guacamole (page 82)
fried onions
roast or piquillo peppers
kimchi, pickled slaw or pickles
spicy mayo (page 35), spicy tomato sauce, barbecue sauce, hot sauce, bacon jam or relish of your choice

Melt the butter in a saucepan, toss in the onions, if using, cover and sweat over a low heat for 5–6 minutes until soft but not coloured. Set aside to get cold.

Meanwhile, mix the beef mince with the herbs and season with salt and pepper. Then add the cooled onions and mix well. Fry off a tiny bit of the mixture in the pan to check the seasoning and adjust if necessary.

With wet hands, shape the mixture into four burgers, or more depending on the size you require. Chill until needed.

Cook to your taste in a little oil in a medium-hot frying or griddle pan, turning once. For rare, cook for 2 minutes each side, for medium 3 minutes and for well done 4 minutes. If you're cooking the burgers in batches, make sure to wash and dry the pan between batches. Burgers can plump up in the centre while being cooked; to avoid this, make an indentation in the centre of each raw burger with your thumb.

Serve with any of the serving suggestions above, or try one of the variations overleaf.

VARIATIONS

* **Cheeseburgers** Lay a slice of cheese on top of each burger and pop under the grill until the cheese begins to melt. Serve as in the main recipe.

* **Beef & mushroom burgers** Heat 1 tablespoon of extra virgin oil in a pan over a high heat. Add 225g (8oz) finely chopped flat or chestnut mushrooms, season well with salt and pepper and cook over a high heat, stirring occasionally, until all the liquid is absorbed. Season to taste, transfer to a plate and leave to get cold. Once cooled, mix the mushrooms with 450g (1lb) minced beef. (You should have about one-quarter mushrooms to three-quarters beef by volume.) Fry off a little morsel to check the seasoning. Shape into four burgers. Cook as in the main recipe and serve with your favourite accompaniments.

* **Beefburgers with ginger mushrooms** Melt 15–25g (½–1oz) butter in a heavy-bottomed saucepan until it foams. Add 75g (3oz) finely chopped onions, cover and sweat over a gentle heat for 5–6 minutes or until quite soft but not coloured. Meanwhile, slice and cook 225g (8oz) flat or chestnut mushrooms in a hot frying pan, in batches if necessary. Season each batch with salt, pepper and a tiny squeeze of lemon juice. Add the mushrooms to the onions in the saucepan, then add 125ml (4fl oz) double cream, 1 teaspoon of freshly grated ginger, 20g (¾oz) nibbed, lightly toasted almonds, if you wish, and allow to bubble for a few minutes. Season to taste, then add 1–2 tablespoons of chopped flat-leaf parsley and ½ tablespoon of freshly chopped chives, if you wish. Set aside.

* To make **Buffalo chips,** scrub 4 large potatoes potatoes and cut them into wedges from top to bottom – they should be about 2cm (¾in) thick and at least 6.5cm (2½in) long. If you like, rinse the chips quickly in cold water but do not soak. Dry them meticulously with a tea towel or kitchen paper before cooking. Deep-fat fryers vary in size so fill the fryer up to the recommended line. Heat dripping or olive oil, or a mixture of olive and sunflower oil, in a deep-fat fryer to 160°C (325°F). Fry twice, once at 160°C (325°F) until they are soft and just beginning to brown, the time will vary from 4–10 minutes depending on the size of the chips. Drain, increase the heat to 190°C (375°F) and cook for a further 1–2 minutes or until crisp and golden. Shake the basket, drain well, toss on to kitchen paper, sprinkle with a little salt, turn into a hot serving dish and serve immediately. Alternatively, fry in a deep saucepan with 5–7.5cm (2–3in) depth of olive oil. Cook the burgers as in the main recipe, transfer on to hot plates, spoon some ginger mushrooms over the burgers and pile on the crispy buffalo chips.

* **Smashburger** (Serves 4) Heat a frying pan or griddle pan over a high heat. Melt 1–2 tablespoons of beef dripping. Divide 450g (1lb) freshly minced beef (20% fat) into four balls. Flatten each down with a spatula or whatever implement you find handy. Smashburgers get their name 'cos you get to smash them flat. Season with sea salt and flatten so the edges are lacy. Cook for a minute or two and when the surface is well browned, flip over. Season the surface with salt and pepper. Lay a very thin slice of melty cheese on top of each burger, then cover the pan with a lid so the cheese starts to melt. Meanwhile, split 4 burger buns in half, slather the surface of each with hot mayonnaise (mayo and tomato ketchup mixed with a dash of hot sauce or Tabasco). Top the base with the smashburger, add a couple of slices of pickled gherkin, maybe some shredded lettuce and a couple of slices of tomato, or whatever you fancy. Top with the other half of the bun. Enjoy right away.

BALLYMALOE HOMEMADE SAUSAGES

Sausages made from 100 per cent lean meat may sound good, but for sweetness and succulence you also need some fat. The addition of breadcrumbs is not just to add bulk, it greatly improves the texture, too.

SERVES 8/MAKES 16 SMALL OR 8 LARGE SAUSAGES

2 tablespoons mixed fresh herbs, such as
   flat-leaf parsley, thyme, chives, marjoram,
   rosemary and sage
60g (2½oz) soft, white breadcrumbs
1 large garlic clove
1 teaspoon salt and freshly ground black pepper
1 organic, free-range egg (optional – helps to
   bind – use 50g/2oz breadcrumbs if omitting egg)
450g (1lb) good, fat streaky pork (rindless),
   minced
dash of olive oil, for frying
50g (2oz) natural sheep or hog casings (optional)

FOR THE BRAMLEY APPLE SAUCE

450g (1lb) Bramley cooking apples
50g (2oz) sugar, or more depending on tartness of
   the apples

Chop the herbs finely and mix through the breadcrumbs. Crush the garlic to a paste with a little salt and add to the breadcrumbs. Whisk the egg, and then mix thoroughly with the breadcrumbs and mince. Season with salt and pepper. Fry off a little knob of the mixture to check the seasoning. Correct if necessary. Fill the mixture into natural sausage casings and tie. Twist into sausages at regular intervals. Alternatively, divide into 16 pieces and roll into lengths to make skinless sausages or shape into rounds for pork burgers or patties. Cover and chill.

Homemade sausages are best eaten fresh but will keep in the fridge for 2–3 days.

To make the apple sauce to serve with sausages, peel, quarter and core the apples, then cut the quarters in two and put in a small stainless-steel or cast-iron saucepan. Add the sugar and 2 teaspoons of water, cover and cook over a low heat. As soon as the apples have broken down, stir so the sauce is a uniform texture and taste for sweetness. Serve warm.

VARIATIONS

✱ Replace the fresh herbs with 1 tablespoon of freshly grated ginger and 4 tablespoons of sliced spring onions.
✱ Add 1 tablespoon of fish sauce to the main recipe.
✱ Add 1 tablespoon of harissa and 2 tablespoons of chopped coriander.
✱ Add 1 tablespoon of freshly ground cumin seeds and 1 tablespoon of freshly ground coriander seeds.

LAMB MEATBALLS WITH YOGURT & MINT

Meatballs are super versatile and a universal comfort food, loved by everyone from the cool kids to grandads. They're good served with flatbreads, rice, couscous, spaghetti or orzo or on a bed of hummus (page 64).

SERVES 6–8

1kg (2lb 4oz) lamb shoulder, freshly minced
150g (5oz) fine white breadcrumbs
2 tablespoons extra virgin olive oil
1 large onion (225g/8oz), finely sliced
3 garlic cloves, finely chopped
1 green chilli, deseeded and finely chopped
2 teaspoons sweet paprika
1 teaspoon ground cumin
1 teaspoon ground coriander
1 teaspoon ground turmeric
2 x 400g (14oz) cans chopped tomatoes or
    900g (2lb) ripe, peeled and chopped tomatoes

200ml (7fl oz) chicken or lamb stock (pages 30–1)
    or water
sea salt, freshly ground black pepper and sugar

TO SERVE

150g (5oz) natural yogurt
thinly sliced red chilli (optional)
a large bunch of mint
2 tablespoons coarsely chopped pistachios
    (optional)

Mix the lamb and breadcrumbs together in a large bowl and season well with salt and pepper. Fry a little bit of the mixture to taste for seasoning and adjust if necessary. Shape into walnut-sized meatballs, weighing 25–30g (1oz) each.

Heat the olive oil in a large sauté pan over a medium heat. Brown the meatballs in batches, being careful not to burn. Remove with a slotted spoon and set aside.

Sweat the onion in the same pan in the leftover oil and fat for 10 minutes over a low heat or until soft. Add the garlic, chilli and spices, stir and cook for 1 minute. Add the tomatoes, season with salt, pepper and sugar and cook for 10 minutes. Pour in the stock, cover the pan and bring gently to the boil. Add the meatballs and simmer for 10–12 minutes until fully cooked (depending on their size). Season to taste.

Serve with blobs of yogurt, with thinly sliced red chilli on top, if you wish. Scatter with lots of torn fresh mint leaves (or mix the torn mint leaves through the yogurt) and pistachios, if using.

VARIATIONS

✳ **Lamb koftas** Shape the lamb mixture into torpedo-shaped koftas or shape around skewers. These are great grilled over charcoal for extra smoky flavour.

HOW TO COOK / MEAT, POULTRY

SLOW-COOKED LAMB BREAST WITH RUSTIC ROASTIES, AIOLI, TOMATO SALSA & ROCKET

One of the Ballymaloe Cookery School tutors, Leo Babin, makes this occasionally for Wednesday lunch at the school – the students love it and plead for the recipe. Lamb breasts are super delicious and really succulent and affordable. Try Pickled cucumber instead of Tomato salsa for another delicious combination.

SERVES 8–10

3 lamb breasts, weighing about 2kg (4lb 8oz)
450ml (16fl oz) lamb stock (page 31)
1.3kg (3lb) maincrop potatoes
a generous drizzle of extra virgin olive oil
1 tablespoon chopped rosemary
flaky sea salt and freshly ground black pepper

TO SERVE

2 handfuls of rocket leaves and/or watercress sprigs
Tomato salsa or Pickled cucumber salad (pages 82 and 34)
Aioli (page 35)
a handful of coarsely chopped flat-leaf parsley

Preheat the oven to 180°C/350°F/gas mark 4.

Score the fat side of the lamb breasts, season with salt and pepper, arrange in a single layer on a tray. Roast for 30 minutes, then reduce the oven temperature to 150°C/300°F/gas mark 2 and cook for 1 hour.

Remove from the oven and rest in a warm place while you make the gravy.

Degrease the tray, remove the fat with a spoon and discard and save the juices. Deglaze the roasting tray with lamb stock and bring to the boil to dissolve all the caramelized juices. Reduce the volume by a third to concentrate the flavour.

Remove the lamb skin and lift off the meat in bite-sized pieces – it will be soft and meltingly tender. Add the reduced jus to the lamb. Discard the excess fat but save the extra juices for the aioli and check the seasoning. Cover and keep warm in the oven until needed.

Put the skin back into the oven on a rack at 160°C/325°F/gas mark 3 for 30–40 minutes until crisp and golden.

Increase the oven temperature to 250°C/500°F/gas mark 10.

Wash the potatoes (no need to peel) and cut into wedges, quarters or sixths depending on size. Toss with extra virgin olive oil and the rosemary.
Lay the potato wedges in a roasting tin in a single layer and season with salt and pepper. Roast for 15–20 minutes until fully cooked, crisp and golden.

To serve, heat the remaining lamb jus. Thin the aioli with the lamb jus to a drizzling consistency. Cover the base of a large serving dish with a layer of rocket and/or watercress sprigs. Drizzle with a little extra virgin olive oil, season with a few flakes of sea salt. Scatter the hot potato wedges and hot pulled lamb over the leaves. Drizzle with the aioli, sprinkle with tomato salsa and scatter crispy pieces of lamb skin over the top. Finally, sprinkle over the parsley and a few flakes of sea salt.

SPICED LAMB PIE

Everyone loves a pie – a tasty filling enrobed in pastry. This particular pastry works brilliantly for both meat and vegetable pies. Puff pastry may be used instead and just follow the same method below. Try adding 2 tablespoons of freshly chopped lovage for a flavour variation.

SERVES 6

450g (1lb) boneless lamb or mutton from the shoulder or leg (keep bones for stock)
2 tablespoons vegetable oil (optional)
250g (9oz) onions, cut into 5mm (¼in) pieces
250g (9oz) carrots, cut into 5mm (¼in) pieces
2 tablespoons plain flour
1 generous teaspoon of both ground cumin and

coriander or 2 teaspoons cumin seeds or
½–1 tablespoon thyme leaves
300ml (10fl oz) lamb or mutton stock (page 31)
1 x quantity Hot water crust pastry (page 25)
1 organic, free-range egg, beaten with a pinch of salt
sea salt and freshly ground black pepper
green salad (page 32), to serve

Trim virtually all the surplus fat from the lamb, then dice the meat into pieces about the size of a small sugar lump. Render down the scraps of fat in a hot, wide sauté pan until the fat runs. Alternatively, use a couple of tablespoons of olive oil. Toss the vegetables in the fat or oil and cook for 3–4 minutes. Remove the vegetables and toss the meat in the remaining fat or oil over a high heat just until the colour changes.

Stir the flour and spices or thyme into the lamb. Cook gently for 2 minutes, then blend the stock in gradually. Bring to the boil, stirring occasionally. Return the vegetables to the pan, season with salt and pepper, cover and simmer for 30 minutes–1 hour. If you're using young lamb, 30 minutes should be ample; an older animal may take up to 1 hour.

Preheat the oven to 220°C/425°F/gas mark 7.

Divide the pastry into two pieces – one about two-thirds of the dough. Roll the larger piece 5mm (¼in) thick to line the base of two 15cm (6in) tins, 4cm (1½in) high, or one 17.5cm (6¾in) tart tin. Save the remaining one-third of the pastry for the lids.

Fill the pastry-lined tins with the cooled lamb mixture. Brush the edges of the pastry with water and press on the pastry lids, pinching them tightly together. Roll out the trimmings to make leaves or twirls to decorate the top(s); make a hole in the centre(s) to allow steam to escape. Brush the lid(s) with the beaten egg and bake the pie(s) for 30–40 minutes on the lower oven rack. Smaller pies will take about 30 minutes.

Serve with a salad of seasonal leaves. This pie or pies freeze perfectly, either cooked or uncooked for 2–3 months, but enjoy sooner rather than later.

VARIATIONS

* **Spiced vegetable pie** Omit the lamb and add 225g (8oz) peeled and chopped potatoes, 225g (8oz) peeled and chopped celeriac, 110g (4oz) peeled and chopped parsnips, 110g (4oz) sliced and sautéed mushrooms, 3 teaspoons of coriander seeds, ½ teaspoon of cardamom seeds and 1 teaspoon of ground turmeric and proceed as in the main recipe.

* **Beef pie** Use Gutsy beef stew (page 148) as a filling.

SWEET TREATS

GREAT-GRANDMOTHER'S VICTORIA SPONGE

This cake keeps brilliantly in a tin for 4–5 days. My great-grandmother would have made all her cakes by hand but a food mixer is a brilliant time-saver and certainly worth investing in to make cakes where possible. This cake can be used as a base for many other confections, filled and iced with a variety of icings.

SERVES 10–12

125g (4½oz) butter, softened, plus extra
   melted for greasing
175g (6oz) plain flour, plus extra for dusting
175g (6oz) caster sugar, plus extra to sprinkle
3 organic and free-range eggs
1 teaspoon baking powder
1 tablespoon whole milk

FOR THE FILLING

110g (4oz) raspberry jam (see below)
300ml (10fl oz) softly whipped cream

Preheat the oven to 190°C/375°F/gas mark 5. Grease two 18cm (7in) cake tins with melted butter, dust with flour and line the base of each with baking parchment.

Cream the butter in a wide bowl, gradually add the sugar and beat until soft and light and quite pale in colour. Add the eggs one at a time and beat well between each addition. (If the butter and sugar are not creamed properly and if the eggs are added too fast, the mixture will curdle, resulting in a cake with a heavier texture.)

Sift the flour and baking powder and stir in gradually. Mix together lightly and add the milk to moisten. It should be a dropping consistency (in other words, the mixture should drop easily from a spoon).

Divide the mixture between the two tins, hollowing it slightly in the centres. Bake for 20–25 minutes – the cakes will shrink slightly from the edges of the tins when fully cooked, the centres should feel exactly the same texture as the edges. Alternatively, a skewer should come out clean when inserted into the centres. Turn out on to a wire rack, remove the baking parchment from the bases, then flip over so the tops of the cakes don't get marked by the wire rack. Leave to cool.

Sandwich the cakes together with the raspberry jam and whipped cream. Sprinkle with sifted caster sugar. Even better, add a layer of fresh raspberries as well as the jam.

VARIATIONS

✱ **Raspberry jam** (Makes 3 x 450g/1lb pots) Heat 790g (1lb 12oz) granulated sugar in the oven at 180°C/350°F/gas mark 4 for 5–10 minutes. Put 900g (2lb) fresh or frozen raspberries into a wide stainless-steel saucepan and cook for 3–4 minutes until the juice begins to run, then add the hot sugar and stir over a gentle heat until fully dissolved. Increase the heat and boil steadily for about 5 minutes, stirring frequently. Test for a set by putting about a teaspoon of jam on a cold plate and leaving it for a few minutes in a cool place. It should wrinkle when pressed with a finger. Remove from the heat immediately. Skim and pour into sterilized jam jars. Cover immediately. Hide the jam in a cool place or else put on a shelf in your kitchen so you can feel great every time you look at it! It will keep for 3 months or more but is best eaten sooner rather than later.

✱ **Rhubarb & ginger jam with cream** Replace the raspberry jam with rhubarb and ginger jam.

MY FAVOURITE CHOCOLATE CAKE

If I had to pick just one chocolate cake, this is it. Claudia Roden, one of my favourite cooks and food writers, showed us how to make this delicious flourless cake when she came to the school for the inaugural Ballymaloe Litfest in 2013. It's her family's favourite chocolate cake, not at all surprising.

SERVES 10 Ⓥ

150g (5oz) dark chocolate (I use 54% Callebaut)
150g (5oz) unsalted butter, diced
4 large, organic, free-range eggs, separated
100g (3½oz) caster sugar
100g (3½oz) ground almonds
1 teaspoon baking powder
4 tablespoons Jamaican rum

FOR THE TOPPING

100g (3½oz) dark chocolate, broken into pieces
  (I use 54% Callebaut)
100g (3½oz) unsalted butter
chocolate curls (optional – see below)
cocoa powder, to dust (optional)

Preheat the oven to 160°C/325°F/gas mark 3 and line a 20.5cm (8in) springform cake tin with baking parchment.

Put the chocolate and 3 tablespoons of water into a heatproof (not stainless-steel) bowl. Sit it on top of a saucepan with a little water over a low heat – the base of the bowl must not touch the water. Bring to the boil, turn off the heat immediately and add the butter. Leave the bowl to sit until the chocolate and butter have melted.

Put the egg yolks, caster sugar, ground almonds, baking powder and rum into a bowl and mix well. Add the melted chocolate and butter and stir vigorously. Whisk the egg whites until stiff and fold gently into the mixture. Pour into the prepared tin. Bake for 35–40 minutes until firm. Leave to cool in the tin and turn out when cool.

Meanwhile, make the topping. Melt the chocolate with the butter in a small bowl over hot water, as before, then mix well. Leave to cool until thick and spreadable. Pour over the cake. Smooth around the sides and top with a palette knife.

Decorate the cake with chocolate curls and dust with cocoa powder, if using. For a very special occasion, sprinkle a few little flakes of gold leaf or edible gold dust on top.

✱ Chocolate curls Melt 150g (5oz) good-quality chocolate with a minimum of 54% cocoa solids (I use Valrhona or Callebaut) in a pan over hot water and stir until smooth. Pour the chocolate over a flat baking sheet and tap the sheet gently to spread. Leave to cool. Once cool, using a cheese slice, or the blade of a chopping knife, pull the blade across the chocolate, creating curls as you go. Use to garnish cakes, mousses or ice cream. Chocolate curls keep for several days in an airtight container.

TUNISIAN ORANGE CAKE

Another must-have recipe, this cake is a real keeper as the syrup preserves the cake for several weeks. It's rich, so serve small helpings for dessert or enjoy as a sweet treat with a cup of coffee.

SERVES 8–10 Ⓥ

200ml (7fl oz) sunflower oil, plus extra for greasing
50g (2oz) slightly stale breadcrumbs
175g (6oz) caster sugar
100g (3½oz) ground almonds
1½ level teaspoons baking powder
4 organic, free-range eggs
finely grated zest of 1 large orange
finely grated zest of ½ lemon
crème fraîche, Greek yogurt or labneh (page 113), to serve

FOR THE ORANGE SYRUP

juice of 1 orange
juice of ½ lemon
50g (2oz) granulated sugar
1 small cinnamon stick
2 cloves

Grease and line a 20.5cm (8in) cake tin, 6.5cm (2½in) deep, with baking parchment.

Mix the breadcrumbs with the sugar, ground almonds and baking powder. Whisk the oil with the eggs, pour into the dry ingredients and mix well. Add the orange and lemon zests. Pour the mixture into the prepared tin.

Put into a cold oven and set the temperature to 180°C/350°F/gas mark 4. Bake for 45–50 minutes for or until the cake looks a rich golden brown. A skewer inserted into the centre should come out clean. Cool for 5 minutes in the tin before turning out on to a plate.

Meanwhile, make the syrup. Put all the ingredients into a stainless-steel saucepan, bring gently to the boil and stir until the sugar has dissolved completely. Simmer for 3 minutes. While it is still warm, pierce holes in the cake with a skewer and pour over the syrup. Leave to cool. Spoon excess syrup back over the cake every now and then until it is all soaked up. You can remove the

cinnamon stick and cloves but I like to leave them on top of the cake.

Serve with a dollop of crème fraîche, thick Greek yogurt or labneh.

VARIATIONS

✱ **Gluten-free Tunisian orange cake**
Substitute gluten-free white breadcrumbs and gluten-free baking powder and proceed as in the main recipe.

✱ **Tunisian lime & lemon cake** Use the juice of 1 lemon and 2 limes, add the zest to the cool syrup and pour over the cake.

✱ **Tunisian orange cake with bergamot syrup** Add the zest and juice of 3 bergamots to the syrup and omit the clove and cinnamon stick.

SIMPLE LEMON DRIZZLE TRAYBAKE

This fantastically useful recipe can be the basis for numerous variations; I do at least twenty riffs on the original lemon drizzle version here, adding myriad flavourings, additions and toppings. Enjoy experimenting with some of the suggestions below. In winter when butter can be harder to cream, I add 2–3 tablespoons of milk to lighten the mixture and texture.

MAKES 24 PIECES

175g (6oz) butter, softened, plus extra for greasing
150g (5oz) caster sugar
2 organic, free-range eggs
175g (6oz) self-raising flour
2–3 tablespoons whole milk (optional)

FOR THE ICING

zest of 1 lemon
juice of 1–2 lemons
110g (4oz) caster sugar

Preheat the oven to 180°C/350°F/gas mark 4. Grease and line a 25.5 x 18cm (10¼ x 7in) Swiss roll tin with baking parchment, allowing the parchment to come up over either ends of the tin for ease of lifting.

Put the butter, sugar, eggs and flour in a food processor. Whizz for a few seconds to amalgamate until the mixture is soft. (Add the milk if the butter is proving hard to cream.) Spread evenly in the tin and bake for 20–25 minutes or until golden brown and well risen.

Meanwhile, mix together all the ingredients for the icing. When the cake is cooked, pour the icing over the top and leave to cool. Cut into squares.

Remove the lemon drizzle squares from the tin if keeping for a few days, unless the tin is coated with Teflon. Best eaten soon but it will still be pretty good in 3–4 days.

VARIATIONS

✻ **Raspberry & coconut traybake** Spread the cooled cake with 350–450g (12oz–1lb) raspberry jam and sprinkle with 50g (2oz) desiccated coconut.

✻ **Blueberry & cinnamon sugar traybake** Scatter 225g (8oz) blueberries evenly over the cake mixture before baking, then proceed as in the main recipe. Mix 50g (2oz) caster sugar with 1–2 teaspoons of ground cinnamon and sprinkle over the cooled cake.

✻ **Orange traybake** Cream 75g (3oz) softened butter with the zest of 2 oranges, add 100g (3½oz) sifted icing sugar and beat until light and fluffy. Spread the icing over the cooled cake. Decorate each square with candied orange peel, if you wish.

✻ **Lemon, pistachio & rose traybake** Add the zest of 1–2 lemons and 1 teaspoon of vanilla extract to the cake mixture and proceed as in the main recipe. Sift 300g (10½oz) icing sugar into a bowl. Add enough lemon juice (plus 1 tablespoon of boiling water if necessary) to mix to a malleable icing and spread over the cake. Sprinkle with 40g (1½oz) chopped pistachios and 1 tablespoon of chopped rose petals.

BEST-EVER CHOCOLATE BROWNIES

Florrie Cullinane, a senior tutor at Ballymaloe Cookery School, shared this recipe, a perennial favourite in her restaurant for over two decades.

MAKES 24–36, depending on size of pieces **V**

375g (13oz) dark chocolate (I use 62% Valrhona
    or Callebaut)
375g (13oz) butter
6 organic, free-range eggs
400g (14oz) caster sugar
200g (7oz) plain flour
150g (5oz) chopped walnuts, hazelnuts or pecans
crème fraîche and/or cherries, to serve (optional)

Preheat the oven to 180°C/350°F/gas mark 4 and line a 35 x 24 x 6cm (14 x 9½ x 2½in) tin with baking parchment.

Melt the chocolate and butter in a heatproof (Pyrex) bowl over a saucepan of barely simmering water.

Whisk the eggs and sugar together to form a light mousse. Gradually add the melted chocolate mixture to the egg mousse. Fold in the flour. Finally, add the chopped nuts. Pour into the prepared tin. Cook for 20 minutes, reduce the oven temperature to 160°C/325°F/gas mark 3 and cook for a further 20 minutes until the centre is slightly wobbly. Leave to cool and set.

Turn out carefully and cut into squares. Serve with crème fraîche and a bowl of fresh cherries, if you wish.

VARIATION

✱ **Pam's vegan chocolate brownies**
(Makes 8–10) Preheat the oven to 180°C/350°F/gas mark 4 and line a 18cm (7in) square tin with baking parchment. Sift 110g (4oz) plain flour, 20g (¾oz) cocoa powder and ¾ teaspoon of baking powder into a bowl. Add 10g (¼oz) desiccated coconut, 80g (3oz) light soft brown sugar, 50g (2oz) golden syrup, 120ml (4fl oz) almond or soya milk and 1 teaspoon of vanilla extract and whisk together. Pour into the tin. You can also scatter 8–10 fresh raspberries or 25g (1oz) toasted coconut flakes over the top before cooking, if you wish. Bake for 20–25 minutes, rotating the tin halfway through the cooking time. A skewer inserted into the centre should come out clean when the brownies are ready. Cool in the tin on a wire rack, then cut into squares.

APPLE & BLACKBERRY PIE

Apple pie is virtually everyone's favourite pudding. My famous break-all-the-rules pastry taught to me by my mum is made by the creaming method, so people who are convinced that they suffer from 'hot hands' don't have to worry about rubbing in the butter. I make this pie year-round with whatever fruits are in season: rhubarb, green gooseberries and elderflower, a mixture of stone fruit, such as apricots, peaches and nectarines... Enjoy all with a blob of softly whipped cream and soft brown sugar, it's obligatory!

SERVES 8–12 **V**

FOR THE BREAK-ALL-THE-RULES PASTRY

225g (8oz) butter, softened
40g (1½oz) caster sugar, plus extra for sprinkling
2 organic, free-range eggs
350g (12oz) plain flour, plus extra for dusting
1 organic, free-range egg, beaten with a dash of milk

FOR THE FILLING

600g (1lb 5oz) Bramley cooking apples, peeled and cut into large dice
110g (4oz) blackberries
150g (5oz) granulated sugar

TO SERVE

softly whipped cream
dark soft brown sugar

Preheat the oven to 180°C/350°F/gas mark 4.

To make the pastry, cream the butter and sugar together by hand or in a food processor. Add the eggs one by one and beat for several minutes. Reduce the speed and mix in the flour slowly. Turn out on to a piece of floured baking parchment, flatten into a round, then wrap and chill. This pastry needs to be chilled for at least 2 hours otherwise it is difficult to handle – better still, make it the day before.

Roll out the pastry to about 3mm (1/8in) thick, then use about two-thirds of it to line a 18 x 30 x 2.5cm (7 x 12 x 1in) square tin or a 22.5cm (8¾in) round tin.

Fill the pie to the top with the apples and blackberries and sprinkle with the sugar. Cover with a lid of pastry, press the edges together to seal. Decorate with pastry leaves, brush with the beaten egg mixture and bake for 45 minutes–1 hour until the apples are tender. When cooked, sprinkle lightly with caster sugar, cut into pieces and serve with softly whipped cream and sugar.

VARIATIONS

* **Classic apple pie** Use 675g (1lb 8oz) Bramley cooking apples, peeled and cut into large dice, 2–3 cloves and 150g (5oz) granulated sugar for the filling.

* **Apple & raspberry pie** Use 450g (1lb) Bramley cooking apples and approx. 225g (8oz) raspberries.

* **Rhubarb pie** Use approx. 900g (2lb) red rhubarb, cut into 1cm (½in) pieces and 175–225g (6–8oz) sugar.

* **Apricot, peach & nectarine pie** Use a total 1kg (2lb 4oz) fruit and 225g (8oz) granulated sugar.

* **Green gooseberry & elderflower pie** Use approx. 700g (1½lb) gooseberries, 250g (9oz) brown sugar and 3 elderflowers.

* **Cherry pie** Use 1kg (2lb 4oz) cherries.

RHUBARB CRUMBLE

Crumbles vie with fruit pies as the top comfort food for all ages and you can vary the fruit according to the season – see some suggestions below. Also try adding 25g (1oz) rolled oats to the crumble instead of the nuts for a different texture.

SERVES 6–8 (V)
700g (1lb 9oz) rhubarb
110g (4oz) granulated sugar

FOR THE CRUMBLE
50g (2oz) cold butter
110g (4oz) plain flour, preferably unbleached
50g (2oz) caster sugar
½ teaspoon ground cinnamon or mixed spice (optional)
25g (1oz) chopped almonds or hazelnuts (optional)

TO SERVE
softly whipped cream
dark soft brown sugar

Preheat the oven to 180°C/350°F/gas mark 4.

Cut the rhubarb into approx. 2.5cm (1in) pieces. Turn into 1.2-litre (2-pint) pie dish. Sprinkle with the sugar.

Rub the butter into the flour just until the mixture resembles really coarse breadcrumbs, add the sugar, and cinnamon and chopped nuts, if using. Sprinkle this mixture over the rhubarb in the pie dish. Bake for 30–45 minutes or until the crumble is cooked and golden.

Serve with whipped cream and soft brown sugar. Or mix the softly whipped cream with chopped crystallized ginger to serve.

VARIATIONS

✳ **Apple crumble** Peel, core and cut 675g (1lb 8oz) Bramley cooking apples into large cubes. Turn into the pie dish and sprinkle with 50g (2oz) granulated sugar. Proceed as opposite.

✳ **Blackberry & apple crumble** Peel, core and cut 600g (1¼lb) Bramley cooking apples into large cubes. Turn into a 1.2-litre (2-pint) pie dish with 110–225g (4–8oz) blackberries and sprinkle with 50g (2oz) granulated sugar and 2 chopped rose geranium leaves (optional).

✳ **Rhubarb & strawberry crumble** Use 450g (1lb) and 250g (9oz) sliced strawberries and proceed as in the main recipe.

✳ **Gooseberry & elderflower crumble** Stew 700g (1½lb) green gooseberries with approx. 300g (10oz) granulated sugar and 2 elderflowers tied in muslin over a medium heat for 3–4 minutes or until they start to burst. Remove the elderflowers and proceed as in the main recipe.

✳ **Plum or apricot crumble** Stew 700g (1½lb) stoned plums or apricots over a medium heat for 3–4 minutes or until they start to burst and proceed as in the main recipe.

✳ **Peach & raspberry crumble** Use 700g (1½lb) peaches and 225g (8oz) raspberries for filling.

✳ **Autumn peach, blueberry & raspberry crumble** Use 700g (1lb 9oz) peaches or nectarines, 225g (8oz) blueberries or 110g (4oz) blueberries and 110g (4oz) raspberries plus 1 tablespoon of cornflour and proceed as in the main recipe.

ALMOND MERINGUE WITH STRAWBERRIES & CREAM

I use this all-in-one meringue recipe for birthdays, anniversaries or simply for a special dessert – it's particularly delicious with raspberries, loganberries, peaches, nectarines or kiwi fruit instead of the strawberries. In winter, I love to use chocolate and rum cream (see below). Doubling the quantities will make four discs for a taller meringue. The meringue discs keep for several weeks in an airtight tin, so can be prepared well in advance and assembled when you need them.

SERVES 6 (V)

45g (1¾oz) whole almonds (or nibbed almonds)
110g (4oz) icing sugar, sifted
2 organic, free-range egg whites
6–8 crystallized rose petals (optional)
little sprigs of mint or lemon balm

FOR THE FILLING

225g (8oz) strawberries (or 110g/4oz raspberries or loganberries)
300ml (10fl oz) softly whipped cream

Blanch and skin the almonds. Grind or chop them up. They should not be ground to a fine powder but should be left slightly coarse and gritty (you could cheat and use nibbed almonds although they won't have as much flavour). Toast in the oven at 180°C/350°F/gas mark 4 for 8–10 minutes until golden.

Reduce the oven temperature to 150°C/300°F/gas mark 2 and mark two 18cm (7in) circles on a sheet of baking parchment.

Check that your mixing bowl is dry, spotlessly clean and free from grease. Add the icing sugar and egg whites and whisk until the mixture forms stiff, dry peaks. Fold the almonds in quickly. Divide the mixture between the two circles and spread evenly with a palette knife.

Bake immediately for 45 minutes or until crisp. Turn off the oven and leave the meringues to cool in the oven. The meringue discs should peel easily off the parchment (which can be reused several times).

Slice the strawberries. Sandwich the meringue discs together with the whipped cream and strawberries, saving a little fruit and cream for decoration. Decorate with the reserved cream and strawberries. Garnish with little sprigs of mint, lemon balm or sweet cicely and/or crystallized rose petals. If you chill for an hour before serving, it will be easier to cut.

VARIATIONS

✳ Almond meringue with peaches & raspberries
Substitute 1 sliced peach and 110g (4oz) raspberries for the strawberries.

✳ Almond meringue with chocolate & rum cream
Melt 25g (1oz) good-quality dark chocolate (62%) and 15g (½oz) unsweetened chocolate (85%) with 1 tablespoon of rum and 1 tablespoon of single cream very gently in a heatproof bowl over a pan of barely simmering water or in a very cool oven. Cool and then fold into 600ml (1 pint) softly whipped cream. Sandwich the meringues together with most of the cream. Decorate with the remaining cream, scattered with halved toasted almonds or chocolate curls (page 165).

LEMON MERINGUE ROULADE

Making a roulade is another fun thing to do with meringue – cook the meringue lightly so it's still soft enough to roll. Fill it with lots of lemon curd and softly whipped cream and whatever else you fancy...

....

SERVES 6–8 **V**

4 organic, free-range egg whites
225g (8oz) caster sugar
sunflower oil, for greasing
300ml (10fl oz) whipped cream
sprigs of mint, lemon balm or sweet cicely, to garnish

FOR THE LEMON CURD
50g (2oz) butter
100g (3½oz) caster sugar
zest and juice of 2 lemons
2 organic, free-range eggs and 1 egg yolk, beaten

FOR THE CRYSTALLIZED LEMON PEEL (optional)
2 lemons
150ml (5fl oz) stock syrup (page 184)
caster sugar, for sprinkling

....

If making the crystallized lemon peel, peel the lemons very thinly with a swivel-top peeler, being careful not to include the white pith, and cut the strips into fine julienne. Put in a saucepan with 450ml (16fl oz) water and simmer for 5 minutes. Remove from the pan, refresh in cold water and repeat the process again. Put the lemon julienne in a saucepan with the stock syrup and cook gently until they look translucent or opaque. Remove with a slotted spoon and leave to cool on baking parchment paper or a wire rack. When cold, sprinkle with caster sugar. The crystallized lemon peel can be stored in a jar or airtight tin for weeks or sometimes months.

Preheat the oven to 180°C/350°F/gas mark 4.

Put the egg whites into the spotlessly clean bowl of a food mixer. Break up with the whisk attachment and then add all the caster sugar in one go. Whisk at full speed for 10–15 minutes until stiff peaks form.

Meanwhile, line a 30.5 x 20.5cm (12¼ x 8in) Swiss roll tin with baking parchment and brush lightly with oil.

Spread the meringue gently over the tin with a palette knife – it ought to be quite thick and bouncy. Bake for 15–20 minutes. Put a sheet of baking parchment on a worktop, turn the roulade out on to it, remove the parchment from the base of the meringue and leave to cool.

Meanwhile, make the lemon curd. Melt the butter over a very low heat, add the sugar, lemon zest and juice and then stir in the well-beaten eggs. Stir carefully over a gentle heat until the mixture coats the back of a spoon. Pour into a bowl (it will thicken as it cools).

To assemble the roulade, spread most of the whipped cream and lemon curd (as much as you like) over the meringue, keeping it 1cm (½in) in from the edge. Roll up from the long side and carefully ease on to a serving plate. Decorate with the reserved cream, crystallized lemon peel and fresh mint, lemon balm or sweet cicely leaves, if using. Serve cut into 2.5cm- (1in-)thick slices and drizzle with a little more lemon curd if desired.

GOOD THINGS WITH ROULADE

* Summer berry roulade Add 225–350g (8–12oz) sliced strawberries or whole raspberries, loganberries, boysenberries, blueberries, wine berries or a mixture to the cream for the filling, reserving a handful of berries to decorate.

* Blackcurrant roulade Add 225–350g (8–12oz) poached blackcurrants to the cream for the filling, reserving a handful of blackcurrants to decorate.

* Pomegranate & rose roulade Add the seeds of 1 pomegranate (reserving a handful of seeds to decorate) and flavour the cream to taste with rose water for the filling.

* Coffee meringue roulade with Irish whiskey cream Make the meringue as in the main recipe, folding in 4 teaspoons of instant coffee powder (not granules) into the meringue before spreading in the tin. Make an Irish whiskey cream by mixing together 300ml (10fl oz) whipped cream and 2 tablespoons Irish whiskey. Spread most of the whiskey cream over the meringue, roll up from the long side and carefully ease on to a serving plate. Decorate with the remaining whiskey cream, chocolate coffee beans and a sprinkling of coffee powder.
For an **Irish coffee sauce** to serve, put the 175g (6oz) granulated sugar and 75ml (3fl oz) water in a heavy-bottomed saucepan; stir until the sugar dissolves and the water comes to the boil. Remove the spoon and do not stir again until the syrup turns a chestnut caramel. Then add 225ml (8fl oz) coffee and put back over the heat to dissolve. Leave to cool and add 1 tablespoon of Irish whiskey. Serve the meringue cut into 2.5cm- (1in-)thick slices accompanied by the Irish coffee sauce.

TUSCAN FRUIT TART

Another of my go-to desserts, I love this recipe not only because it tastes delicious but because it's so versatile and easy to make if you have a food processor. Greengages or apples also work very well.

SERVES 10–12 Ⓥ

175g (6oz) granulated sugar
450g (1lb) plums or apricots, halved and stoned
150g (5oz) butter, softened
150g (5oz) caster sugar
200g (7oz) self-raising flour
3 organic, free-range eggs
1–2 tablespoons whole milk (optional)
crème fraîche or softly whipped cream, to serve

Preheat the oven to 160°C/325°F/gas mark 3.

Put the sugar and 110ml (3¾fl oz) water into a 25.5cm (10¼in) sauté or a cast-iron frying pan. Stir over a medium heat until the sugar dissolves, then cook without stirring until the sugar caramelizes to a rich golden brown (if the caramel is not dark enough the tart will be too sweet). Remove from the heat and arrange the fruit, cut-side down, in a single layer over the caramel. Work fast...and careful not to burn your fingers!

Put the butter, sugar and flour into the bowl of a food processor. Whizz for a second or two, add the eggs and stop as soon as the mixture comes together. (Add the milk if the eggs are small – the mixture should be soft.) Spoon over the fruit, spread gently in as even a layer as possible.

Bake for about 1 hour. The centre should be firm to the touch and the edges slightly shrunk from the sides of the pan. Leave to rest in the pan for 4–5 minutes before turning out. Serve with crème fraîche or softly whipped cream.

BEST-EVER CORNMEAL PANCAKES WITH BUTTER & MAPLE SYRUP

These pancakes inspired by Chez Ma Tante in Brooklyn, New York, are the most delicious I've ever tasted, so I wanted to share them with you. This recipe uses coarse polenta, also known as polenta bramata, or more commonly as cornmeal in the US.

....

MAKES 8 PANCAKES

175g (6oz) plain flour
175g (6oz) coarse polenta (cornmeal)
2 tablespoons caster sugar
1 organic, free-range egg, plus 1 egg yolk
1 teaspoon salt
1½ tablespoons baking powder
2 tablespoons melted butter
300ml (10fl oz) whole milk
225g (8oz) clarified butter (page 15)
butter and maple syrup, to serve

....

Put the flour, polenta and sugar into a bowl. Whisk the egg and egg yolk together and add the salt and baking powder. Stir into the dry ingredients with a wooden spoon, along with the melted butter. Don't beat the mixture – it can still be slightly lumpy.

Heat a heavy cast-iron pan over a medium-high heat for 4–5 minutes. Pour in a generous 3mm (⅛in) of clarified butter and allow to heat through. Pour about 60ml (4 tablespoons) batter into the pan for each pancake and allow some space between each one. Cook for 3–4 minutes until bubbles rise and burst and the edges start to crisp. Flip over carefully and continue to cook on the other side for about 2–3 minutes until both sides are nicely brown and crisp at the edges. You will probably get about two pancakes in the pan at a time, so will need to cook them in batches until you have used all of the batter.

Serve immediately on warm plates allowing two pancakes per person. Slather some butter on each one and drizzle a little maple syrup over the top. Quite simply sublime!

BASIC CRÊPES

This is definitely a top ten essential recipe, made with basic ingredients you'll virtually always have in your pantry. It's my go-to when I want to whip up something delicious in minutes. I often cook the crêpes right away but for even better results allow the batter to stand for a while if time permits.

....

SERVES 6 / MAKES APPROX. 12

175g (6oz) plain flour
a good pinch of salt
1 dessertspoon caster sugar, plus
    1 tablespoon (optional)
2 large, organic, free-range eggs, plus 1 or 2 egg yolks

scant 450ml (16fl oz) whole milk, or for very crisp,
    light delicate pancakes, milk and water mixed
zest of ½ lemon (optional)
3–4 dessertspoons melted butter, plus
    extra for greasing
caster sugar and lemon wedges, to serve

....

To make the batter, put all the ingredients into a food processor and whizz for a minute or two. Alternatively, sift the flour, salt and sugar into a bowl, make a well in the centre and drop in the lightly beaten eggs. With a whisk or wooden spoon, starting in the centre, mix the egg and gradually bring in the flour. Add the milk slowly and beat until the batter is covered with bubbles. (If you are serving with sugar and lemon juice, stir in an extra tablespoon of caster sugar and the lemon zest.)

If time allows, let the batter stand in a cold place for an hour or so – longer will do no harm. Just before you cook the crêpes, stir in the melted butter. This will make all the difference to the flavour and texture and means you can cook them without greasing the pan each time.

Heat a 20cm (8in) non-stick crêpe pan until very hot. Grease the pan lightly with butter and pour in just enough batter to cover the base of the pan thinly. A small ladle can also be very useful for this. Loosen the crêpes around the edges, flip over with a spatula or thin egg slice, cook for a second or two on the other side, and slide off the pan on to a plate. The crêpes may be stacked on top of each other and peeled apart later. The greasing of the pan is only necessary for the first two or three pancakes.

Serve each crêpe with butter, a sprinkling of caster sugar and a wedge of lemon. Cooked crêpes will keep in the fridge for several days and also freeze perfectly. If they are to be frozen, it's probably a good idea to put a disc of baking parchment between each one for extra safety.

....

VARIATIONS

✱ **Crêpes with orange butter** Cream 175g (6oz) butter with 3 teaspoons of finely grated orange zest. Add 175g (6oz) sifted icing sugar and beat until fluffy. (A tablespoon of orange liqueur, such as Grand Marnier or orange curaçao, is very good added to the orange butter if you are feeling very extravagant!) To serve, melt a blob of the orange butter in the pan, add some freshly squeezed orange juice and toss the crêpes in the foaming butter. Fold in half and then in quarters (fan shapes). Serve 2–3 per person on warm plates. Spoon the buttery orange juices over the top. Repeat until all the crêpes and butter have been used.

✱ **Crêpes with chocolate spread** Spread a little chocolate spread over each crêpe, top with softly whipped cream and a sprinkling of chopped toasted hazelnuts. Fold into a fan and enjoy immediately.

OLD-FASHIONED RICE PUDDING

A creamy rice pudding is delicious just as it is. You need to use short-grain rice, which plumps up as it cooks. This is definitely a forgotten pudding and it's unbelievable the reaction we get to it every time we make it here at the cookery school. Everyone squabbles over the irresistible golden skin and wonders why they don't make it more often.

SERVES 6–8 **V**

100g (3½oz) short-grain rice
40g (1½oz) granulated sugar
small knob of butter
850ml (1½ pints) whole milk

TO SERVE (optional)

softly whipped cream and dark soft brown sugar
vanilla ice cream (page 182)
fruit compote (page 185)

Preheat the oven to 180°C/350°F/gas mark 4.

Put the rice, sugar and butter into a 1.2-litre (2-pint) pie dish. Bring the milk to the boil and pour over the top. Bake for 1¼–1½ hours (usually the latter but keep checking). The skin should be golden, the rice underneath should be cooked through and have absorbed the milk, but the rice pudding should still be soft and creamy. Calculate the time so that it's just ready to serve for pudding. If it has to wait in the oven for ages it will be dry and dull and you may wonder why you bothered.

Serve with softly whipped cream and dark soft brown sugar (best of all!), a scoop of vanilla ice cream melting into the centre or one of the fruit compotes.

VARIATIONS

✳ **Coconut milk rice pudding** Omit the butter and replace the milk with coconut milk for a vegan alternative.

✳ **Sugar-free coconut rice pudding**
(Serves 6–8) Soak 225g (8oz) short-grain brown rice overnight in water with 1–2 tablespoon of whey if available. The next day, preheat the oven to 180°C/350°F/gas mark 4. Add 400ml (14fl oz) coconut milk, 350ml (12fl oz) water, 1–2 tablespoons of whey (optional), 50g (2oz) honey, 1 teaspoon of vanilla extract, 25g (1oz) butter, 50g (2oz) raisins or sultanas, ¼ teaspoon of crushed cardamom seeds and ¼ teaspoon of salt to the rice mixture in a low-sided saucepan. Stir well and bring to the boil, then transfer to a 1.2-litre (2-pint) pie dish. Cover with baking parchment and bake for 2 hours. Serve with softly whipped cream and chopped pistachios.

BALLYMALOE VANILLA ICE CREAM

This recipe is made on an Italian egg-mousse base with really good softly whipped cream. It produces a deliciously rich, smooth ice cream and needs no further whisking during freezing. Remove it from the freezer at least 10 minutes before serving. Lots of other flavourings can be added: liquid ingredients such as melted chocolate or coffee should be folded into the mousse before adding the cream. For chunkier ingredients, such as chocolate chips or raisins soaked in rum, semi-freeze the ice cream and then stir them through, otherwise they will sink to the bottom.

SERVES 12–16 (V)

100g (3½oz) granulated sugar
4 organic, free-range egg yolks
1 teaspoon vanilla extract or seeds from ⅓ vanilla pod
1.2 litres (2 pints) softly whipped double cream
    (measured after it is whipped, for accuracy)

Combine the sugar with 200ml (7fl oz) water in a small, heavy-bottomed saucepan.

Meanwhile, put the egg yolks into a bowl and whisk until light and fluffy (keep the whites for meringues, page 175).

Stir the sugar and water mixture over a medium heat until the sugar is completely dissolved, then remove the spoon and boil the syrup until it reaches the 'thread' stage, about 106–113°C (223–235°F): it will look thick and syrupy, and when a metal spoon is dipped in, the last drops of syrup will form thin threads. Pour this boiling syrup in a steady stream on to the egg yolks, whisking all the time by hand. (If you are whisking the mousse in a food processor, remove the bowl and whisk the boiling syrup in by hand; otherwise it will solidify on the sides of the bowl.)

Add the vanilla extract or seeds and continue to whisk the mixture until it becomes a thick, creamy white mousse. This is the stage at which, if you're deviating from this recipe, you can add liquid flavourings such as coffee. Fold the softly whipped cream into the mousse, pour into a freezerproof bowl or box, cover and freeze.

FUN WAYS TO SERVE ICE CREAM

✱ Ice-cream cones Scoop the ice cream into ice-cream cones and enjoy just as it is or with your favourite sprinkle.

✱ Ice-cream sundae Combine 2–3 scoops of ice cream in a sundae glass, drizzle with fruit sauce or coulis or hot chocolate sauce and toasted nuts, caramel popcorn, salted peanuts or sprinkles. To make hot chocolate sauce, melt 50g (2oz) dark chocolate and 25g (1oz) unsweetened chocolate in a heatproof bowl over a saucepan of simmering water or in a low oven. Gradually stir in 175ml (6fl oz) warm stock syrup (page 184). Flavour with 1 tablespoon of rum or 1 teaspoon of vanilla extract. Serve warm.

✱ Choc ices Slice the block of ice cream, dip in cool melted chocolate and refreeze on parchment paper to make your own delicious choc ices.

✱ Affogato Add a scoop of vanilla ice cream to a shot of espresso in an espresso cup or small glass.

✱ Vanilla ice cream with Pedro Ximénez raisins Cover 100g (3½oz) raisins with 100ml (3½fl oz) Pedro Ximénez sherry or Pedro Ximénez Malaga wine. Drizzle a little Pedro Ximénez raisins over the ice cream on the plate just before you tuck in.

ICE-CREAM CONES

ICE-CREAM SUNDAE

CHOC ICES

AFFOGATO

FLAVOUR-PACKED FRUIT FOOLS

Why 'fool'? Well, you could say because fools are so easy to make, any fool could whip them up, but apparently the word comes from the French verb 'fouler' – to crush. They can be made from a variety of fruit but blackcurrants, gooseberries and rhubarb need to be cooked and puréed first.

BLACKCURRANT FOOL

Frozen blackcurrants tend to be less sweet so you will need to add extra sugar. The fool should not be very stiff, more like the texture of softly whipped cream. If it is too stiff, stir in a little milk rather than more cream.

SERVES 6 Ⓥ

300ml (10fl oz) double cream
350g (12oz) blackcurrants, fresh or frozen
200ml (7fl oz) stock syrup (see below)
shortbread biscuits, to serve

FOR THE STOCK SYRUP (Makes 825ml/1½ pints)
450g (1lb) granulated sugar

To make the stock syrup, dissolve the sugar in 600ml (1 pint) water and bring to the boil. Boil for 2 minutes, then leave it to cool. Store in the fridge until needed.

Sofly whip the cream in a bowl.

Cover the blackcurrants with the stock syrup. Bring to the boil and cook for 4–5 minutes until the fruit bursts. Liquidize and sieve or purée the mixture and measure it. When the purée has cooled, add the cream to taste, start with about half cream to blackcurrant purée – the texture should be soft and flowing rather than too stiff. Taste, it may need more sugar depending on the variety. Divide between six bowls. Alternatively, you can layer the purée and cream in tall sundae glasses, ending with a drizzle of thin purée over the top. Serve with shortbread biscuits.

VARIATIONS

✱ **Green gooseberry & elderflower fool** Use 450g (1lb) green gooseberries and 3–4 elderflower heads (tied in muslin), cover in stock syrup made from 175g (6oz) granulated sugar and 300ml (10fl oz) water. Add softly whipped cream to taste – about half the volume of the gooseberries.

✱ **Rhubarb fool** Use 450g (1lb) red rhubarb, cut into chunks. Cover in stock syrup made from 175g (6oz) granulated sugar and 2 tablespoons of water. Fold in 225–300ml (8–10fl oz) softly whipped cream to taste.

✱ **Damson fool** Cook 1kg (2¼lb) damsons in 225ml (8fl oz) of stock syrup (see above) and proceed as in the main recipe.

✱ **Rory's raspberry fool** (Serves 8–10) Scatter 450g (1lb) fresh or frozen raspberries over a dish or tray. Sprinkle over 150–175g (5–6oz) caster sugar and leave to macerate for 1 hour. If you are using frozen berries, this should be long enough for them to defrost. Purée the fruit in a liquidizer or blender. Pass the purée through a sieve to remove the seeds. Discard the seeds. Gently fold in 600ml (1 pint) whipped cream. If you wish to create a swirly effect, just be a little light-handed with the folding in of the cream. The fool is now ready to be served or can be chilled for serving later that day. Serve with shortbread biscuits. Freeze any leftover fool, it makes a delicious raspberry ice cream.

MY FAVOURITE FRUIT COMPOTES

Compote is the term used for seasonal fruit poached gently in syrup. There are lots of variations and, of course, complementary herbs and spices can be used to flavour the syrup – experiment with the alternatives below depending on what fruit is in season.

BLACKBERRY & APPLE COMPOTE

A delicious autumn dessert. Wild or cultivated blackberries can be used here. It will taste even better and is such fun if you pick the wild fruit from the hedgerows yourself.

SERVES APPROX. 3 Ⓥ

195g (7oz) granulated sugar
8 large rose geranium leaves
4 large dessert apples, such as Worcester Pearmain or Cox's Orange Pippin
275g (10oz) blackberries, wild or cultivated
shortbread biscuits, to serve

Put the sugar, 450ml (16fl oz) cold water and the rose geranium leaves into a saucepan and bring to the boil for 1–2 minutes. Peel the apples thinly with a peeler, keeping a good round shape. Quarter them, remove the core and trim the ends. Cut into segments 5mm (¼in) thick. Add to the syrup. Cover with a paper lid and the lid of the saucepan and poach for 6-8 minutes (depending on the variety) until translucent but not broken.

Just 3–5 minutes before they have finished cooking, add the blackberries and simmer together so that they are both cooked at once.

Serve chilled, with little shortbread biscuits. This compote keeps deliciously, covered in a fridge for up to a month – I love it with ice cream (page 182), panna cotta, crème caramel or labneh (page 113).

VARIATIONS

✳ **Cranberry & apple compote** Substitute 275g (10oz) cranberries for blackberries in the main recipe.

✳ **Green gooseberry & elderflower compote** (Serves 6–8) Top and tail 900g (2lb) hard, green gooseberries. Put in a stainless-steel or enamel saucepan, add 400g (14oz) granulated sugar and cover with 600ml (1 pint) water. Tie 2 or 3 large elderflower heads in a little square of muslin. Add to the saucepan, bring slowly to the boil and continue to boil for 2 minutes. Add the gooseberries and simmer for 6–8 minutes – just until the fruit bursts. Leave to get cold. Flavour softly whipped cream to taste with elderflower cordial and serve alongside. This compote should keep perfectly in the fridge for up to 2 weeks. It's also delicious served with roast duck (page 145) or pork.

✳ **Myrtle's Pear Compote** (Serves 6) Halve 6 ripe pears, peel thinly and core carefully, keeping a good shape. Put them in a pan which will just fit them nicely. Add 110g (4oz) granulated sugar, a few thin strips of lemon rind and the juice of 1 lemon. Cover with a well-fitting lid and cook gently for 20–30 minutes until soft. Cool and serve alone or with softly whipped cream. This compote keeps brilliantly in the fridge for a week or more.

MEAL IDEAS

WEEKEND BRUNCH

Huevos rancheros (page 106)

Toasted nut & grain granola (page 40)

A classic French omelette (pages 14–15)

Flexible frittata (page 108)

Baked eggs (page 100)

Scrambled eggs (page 102)

Ballymaloe seasonal muesli (page 42)

COOKING TO IMPRESS

Baked flat fish with herb butter (page 119)
Almond meringue with strawberries & cream
(page 175)

Crispy duck legs with onions & rosemary (page 145)
Tunisian orange cake (page 166)

Stir-fried prawns & pork with crispy noodles
(page 132)
Tuscan fruit tart (page 177)

Slow-cooked lamb breast with rustic roasties,
aioli, tomato salsa & rocket (page 157)
My favourite chocolate cake (page 165)

YOUR MEAL PLANNERS

KITCHEN SUPPERS

Everyday dhal (page 48)

Simple spaghetti & meatballs (page 55)

Veggie toad in the hole (page 71)

Basic beefburgers (pages 151–2)

Seasonal vegetable & paneer curry (page 80)

Rhubarb crumble (page 172)

Flavour-packed fruit fools (page 184)

SIMPLE LUNCHES

A simple soup (page 20)
Simple lemon drizzle traybake (page 167)

Quesadilla foldies (page 82)
Best-ever chocolate brownies (page 168)

Salad Niçoise with tuna (page 130)
Basic crêpes (page 180)

Roast squash & spelt salad (page 43)
My favourite fruit compotes (page 185)

INDEX

SO MANY THANK YOUS, YET AGAIN.

This book of '100 recipes no one should leave school' without is my twentieth book, the cookbook I always said I must write before I hang up my apron. But now that I've completed the manuscript, there are several other ideas buzzing around in my head so who knows, perhaps there will be a twenty-first...

A very special thank you to Sharon Hogan who had the mammoth task of typing and retyping my handwritten recipes with occasional help from Kate Fleming.

Gary Masterson did the lion's share of the recipe testing in the midst of teaching and cooking for the farmers' markets. Several other BCS tutors – Tiffin Griffin, Florrie Cullinane, Pamela Black and Patrick Browne – also lent a hand from time to time and offered sage advice from their long years of experience.

Joanna Copestick and Kyle Books have been ever supportive and patient, even when I missed my deadline once again...

And yet another thank you to my agent Heather Holden-Brown for constant cheerful support and advice.

My editor, Vicky Orchard, who has been heroic as ever. This is the fifth book we've worked on together. Thank you from the bottom of my heart, particularly for your seemingly endless patience.

A big shout out to the design, sales and marketing team who also worked their magic behind the scenes.

Such beautiful photos, thank you Nassima Rothacker for bringing my book to life and to Annie Rigg and Morag Farquhar for making my food look so mouth-wateringly delicious. The idea is to tempt you to dash into the kitchen... And to my daughter, Lydia Hugh-Jones, for the evocative illustrations.

And last but not least, a huge and sincere thanks to Tim, all my extended family and the Ballymaloe Cookery School team for their constant support and encouragement, particularly during these challenging times.